NATURALLY
HEALTHY
CATS

Dr. Carol Osborne

MARSHALL PUBLISHING • LONDON

A Marshall Edition
Conceived, edited and designed by
Marshall Editions Ltd
The Orangery
161 New Bond Street
London W1Y 9PA

First published in the UK in 1999 by
Marshall Publishing Ltd

ISBN: 1 84028 287 8

Originated in Singapore by Pica
Printed and bound in China by Excel

Author Dr. Carol Osborne
Consultant David Alderton
Project Editor Sadie Smith
Art Editor Patrick Carpenter
Managing Editor Conor Kilgallon
Designer Sue Storey
Copy Editor Lindsay McTeague
Indexer Jill Dormon
Picture Research Antonella Mauro
Editorial Director Ellen Dupont
Art Director Dave Goodman
Editorial Coordinator Ros Highstead
Production Amanda Mackie

Note
Every effort has been taken to ensure that
all information in this book is correct and
compatible with national standards generally
accepted at the time of publication. This book
is not intended to replace consultation with your
veterinarian or complementary therapy
practitioner. The author and publisher disclaim
any liability, loss, injury or damage incurred as a
consequence, directly or indirectly, of the use and
application of the contents of this book.

CONTENTS

The Head

The Digestive System

Skin and Hair

Systemic Illnesses

Behavioural Problems

First Aid

INTRODUCTION

As veterinary science and understanding of bodily function improves, our pets are able to live longer and healthier lives. Cats now often live into their twenties because of better sanitation and treatment of infectious disease. You can help your cat enjoy this longer life by paying attention to its nutrition and its general state of health and enabling your vet to act right from the start of any illness. This factfile tells you how to care for your cat, how to recognize when it needs veterinary treatment and how to care for it at home when it is ill.

No one form of medicine has all the answers. We now realize that stress and anxiety can affect our pets as much as it does ourselves. Parallel with improvements in veterinary science has been a growth in complementary medicine whose qualified practitioners offer a range of treatments for pets. This book tells you about complementary treatments, notably herbal remedies and homeopathy. These treatments will often help to alleviate the symptoms of illness and make your pet feel more comfortable, but they are not a substitute for veterinary advice. If you are worried about your cat's health, you should always contact your vet. The sooner you seek advice, the quicker your cat will feel better.

USING THE FACTFILE

The book is divided into six chapters: 1 The Head; 2 The Digestive System; 3 Skin and Hair; 4 Systemic Illnesses; 5 Behavioural Problems; 6 First Aid. If you know which subject you wish to look up, then simply turn to the relevant tab, the colour coded dividers. On each divider, you will find a table of contents for that part of the book. If you are unsure where to find the information you need, turn to the alphabetical index on page 112.

TEXT AND ILLUSTRATIONS

The text for each ailment is clearly divided into a description of the problem, its causes and what a vet might do to treat it. How you can help your pet, not only during its illness but also by improving its lifestyle so that it is less susceptible to illness in the first place, is also discussed. Anatomical drawings as well as photographs amplify and complement the text.

The book is not intended to be used instead of advice from your veterinarian, but to encourage greater understanding of natural health.

CHOOSING A VET

When you are choosing a vet, your initial reaction is generally your best guide. You need to find a person with whom you feel confident and comfortable and who is also conveniently located. It is advisable to register with a vet soon after acquiring your cat so that it can receive a health check and vaccinations can be discussed.

To help you with your choice, you can first check the vet's credentials—they can have a range of qualifications. You can ask for references and pay the practice a visit. One that is close to your home will make life easier for you, particularly in an emergency. Find out the surgery hours—they may be important if you are working.

Second, make sure that the vet can offer all the services you may need: boarding, grooming, hospitalization and 24-hour emergency care. Although you may prefer that your pet always sees the same vet, a group practice often offers specialization in areas that may include alternative medicine. There will also be a greater number of vets available for consultation which you may consider an advantage.

A list of complementary veterinary medical associations that can refer you to qualified practitioners can be found on page 111. There are also internet sources given.

HOW DO I GET THE BEST FROM MY VET?

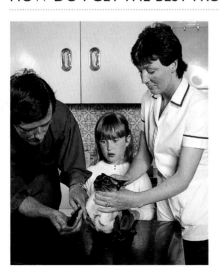

When you need to consult a vet, it is often easy to overlook matters of concern, so it is a good idea to jot down a few notes to take with you. These should cover topics such as:

• Your cat's origins, age and history.

• The signs of illness.

• When symptoms first appeared, and whether your cat has suffered from anything similar in the past.

• Any medications your cat is currently taking.

HOLISTIC MEDICINE

R esearch has shown that health is influenced by physical, mental and emotional factors. Holistic medicine, also known as alternative medicine, aims to take all these factors into account. Herbalism, homeopathy, acupuncture, chiropractic, flower essences and naturopathy are all elements of holistic medicine available for pets. They are not meant to replace conventional veterinary medicine but these therapies are used with it to give your cat the best of both worlds.

HERBALISM

Herbalism is probably the oldest form of medicine. Herbal immune therapy is used to stimulate the immune system to fight disease. You should always consult an experienced practitioner as, wrongly used, herbs can produce unwanted side effects. As a general rule, home-grown or bought fresh herbs should be used. To disguise the taste, you should chop them up and mix them into your cat's food, or they can be made into infusions, dips and tonics.

HOMEOPATHIC REMEDIES

Homeopathists believe that administering an extremely dilute form of a substance similar to the one causing the symptoms stimulates the body to overcome the illness itself. The remedies used are all natural substances and are derived from plants, minerals, or animal products. They are carefully diluted to specific strengths and can be bought in the recommended dilution to be given according to specific guidelines. For cats, they can be given as pellets or crushed to powder and mixed with milk. The cat should not eat any food 10 minutes before or after taking the remedy.

USE WITH CARE !

Although complementary remedies are generally safe, they should be used carefully. Seek veterinary advice before giving any medication to your cat, to ensure that its condition has been diagnosed correctly and that the best course of treatment has been chosen. Some common herbs for example can have cross reactions or side effects which you may not be aware of. Also, homeopathic remedies should not be used with acupuncture or strong herbal tinctures. For the best result, work as a team with your vet and complementary practitioner.

OTHER TREATMENTS

A number of complementary approaches are useful with cats. You should always seek treatment from skilled practitioners in the field of alternative veterinary medicine.

FLOWER ESSENCES

Flower essences are diluted flower preparations that are used to treat behavioural problems, fears, and other psychological disturbances, especially those associated with stress. They help to rebalance mental and emotional well-being. Originally, Edward Bach, a British physician in the 1930s, developed 38 different flower essences, each of which addressed a specific emotional situation. Today they are known as bach flower remedies. Rescue Remedy is one of the most popular. It is a mixture of five flower essences and is commonly used after a phyiscal or emotional trauma or during a stressful situation. For example, if your cat is stressed by the introduction of a new pet into the home, place three drops in or on its mouth or tongue two or three times a day.

ACUPUNCTURE

An ancient Chinese therapy that uses very fine needles to stimulate the body's immune system to heal itself and restore the natural balance of the body. It also stimulates the release of the body's own natural painkillers, the endorphins. Acupuncture has been used on pets for bone problems which cause pain, asthma, long-term digestive problems and epilepsy. The relief, however, is generally temporary and eight or more treatments are often necessary for positive results. Acupuncture should not be used in conjunction with homeopathy.

CHIROPRACTIC

Chiropractic is a drugless therapy in which the spinal cord is manipulated or realigned to relieve pain and restore movement and function after an accident or broken limb. It is generally used with acupuncture, herbal and homeopathic remedies.

NATUROPATHY

Naturopathists believe illness is caused by a build-up of toxins in the body due to poor nutrition and lack of exercise. They recommend a regime of good nutrition and exercise combined with bathing, massage and sunshine.

GLANDULAR THERAPY

These are biologically active nutritional supplements given as treats or mixed with food. Many contain hormonal material from glands, e.g. thyroid, and are used to stimulate a weakened gland to function normally. When used correctly there are no side effects.

THE HEAD

*Cats are susceptible to infections of the
upper part of the respiratory tract. These
can spread to other parts of the body,
particularly into the chest, where the effects
can be severe. Regular vaccinations—which
should be repeated annually throughout the
cat's life to give full protection—will prevent
serious infections, such as the feline
rhinotracheitis virus, occurring.
Anatomically, many parts of a cat's head are
linked so, when a problem
strikes, several areas can be
affected. For this reason,
veterinary advice is
important in order to
diagnose and treat the cause
of the disorder early on. The
head, and specifically the
eyes, can give a clear
indication of a cat's
overall state of health.*

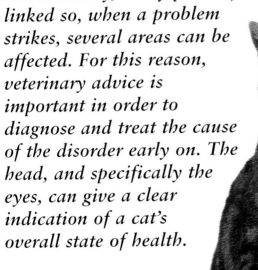

CAT FLU

Cat flu is usually caused by viruses that attack the upper respiratory system. It may be followed by infection of the lungs and pneumonia. These viruses are very contagious. They are transmitted by cat-to-cat contact, by sneezing and coughing, and are responsible for 90 percent of upper respiratory infections in cats. Even those cats that are lucky enough to survive this type of respiratory infection may never make a full recovery, displaying intermittent signs such as a persistent nasal discharge for the rest of their lives. It is therefore sensible to protect your cat by vaccinating it against the main infections that display the typical symptoms of cat flu. Kittens are the most susceptible and without protection can either die or end up with permanent damage to the respiratory tract. Adult cats may only get the common cold for 7–10 days and then recover.

CAUSES

• Cat flu is a general term used to describe feline upper respiratory tract infections. The two most significant viruses implicated in cases of cat flu are feline viral rhinotracheitis (FVR) and feline calici virus (FCV). Both these viruses are contagious. FVR is usually the more serious.

• Less serious symptoms usually result from infection by feline chlamydia, a microbe that is intermediate in structure between a bacterium and a virus—it can be treated successfully by means of tetracycline antibiotics.

• Some cats, while showing no signs of disease, may become flu carriers after contracting feline herpes virus (FHV).

SYMPTOMS

• Sneezing and runny eyes.
• Nasal discharge: clear at first, becoming thicker.
• Increase in temperature.
• Loss of appetite and cat appears tired and listless.
• Breathing may become difficult.
• Ulceration of the tongue and mouth.
• Pneumonia may develop.

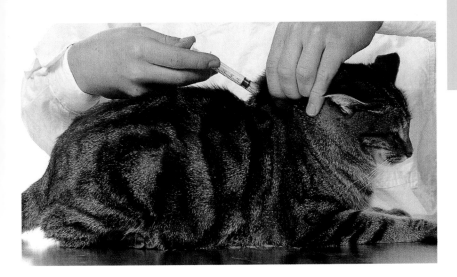

WHAT YOUR VET CAN DO

• Vaccines help to protect your cat against many of the most serious and potentially fatal diseases caused by bacteria and viruses. Cats are most susceptible as kittens so vaccination should be begun at six weeks of age. The shots are given every three to seven weeks until the kitten is 15 weeks old and once a year after that. The most important vaccines are feline upper respiratory tract disease (flu), feline panleukopenia, feline leukaemia and rabies (where appropriate). The first three are usually administered as one shot. All these diseases are fatal, especially in kittens, so you should always keep up with vaccines.

• Antibiotics are often prescribed to reduce the chances of a secondary bacterial infection developing. The vet will explain how they are to be given, usually orally. Good nursing care is important to keep your cat comfortable, so your vet will probably advise you to bathe its eyes regularly to stop them becoming gummed up and to wipe its nose frequently. Take care to dispose of used tissues and cotton balls and wash your hands well afterward.

COMPLEMENTARY TREATMENTS

⊠ HERBAL REMEDIES
A little almond oil on a cotton ball two or three times daily can relieve discomfort in the nasal area.
Calendula tincture, two drops in 25 ml (1 fl oz) of olive oil, can also be applied.

▢ HOMEOPATHIC REMEDIES
Nosodes are homeopathic vaccines made from natural disease products sterilized and diluted. Nosodes are given by mouth over a period of time and stimulate the cat's immune system. They are available for flu, feline panleukopenia, leukaemia and FIP.
Kali bichromicum 200c can ease nasal congestion. Recommended courses usually run over a period of a month.

RUNNY EYES

Your cat's eyes should normally be clear and bright, and free of any discharge. If problems occur, you should consult your vet—eyes are extremely sensitive and improper treatment can result in visual impairment. Cats have three eyelids: upper, lower and another which begins at the inside corner of the eye and is really a membrane. This moves across the eye like a windshield wiper. The most common cause of runny eyes is conjunctivitis—inflammation of the lining of the eye. This and trauma, such as a foreign body in the eyes, can increase the output of tear fluid which in some cases can overflow.

CAUSES

• Allergies. These can be very hard to determine.

• Foreign particles (hair, dust and other irritants) in the eye will increase the flow of tear fluid.

• A particle of grit in the eye or may lead to a corneal lesion or this can sometimes result from a cat fight.

• Infections, viral or bacterial, including feline upper respiratory tract infection and feline panleukopenia.

• With long-haired cats, if hair on the side of the face gets in the eyes it can cause irritation and corneal ulcers.

• The compact facial shape of Persian longhairs often affects the drainage of tear fluid. Instead of flowing freely down the ducts, it runs out over the lower lid and stains the fur in the corner of each eye.

SYMPTOMS

• Runny eyes with clear, watery or thick mucus discharge.
• Red itchy crusty eyes.
• Third eyelid partially covers eye or eyes.
• Tear staining often close to the nose.
• Cat rubs affected eye(s) with its paws.

Overflowing tears are often the result of an inherited defect in the case of flat-faced breeds such as the Persian.

WHAT YOU AND YOUR VET CAN DO

• At the first sign of conjunctivitis wipe the discharge from the eyelids with a warm, moist cloth or cotton balls which can be discarded. You can then give herbal eye drops of cucumber juice, three drops three times daily. Moisten a cotton ball and squeeze the drops into the eye.

• Your vet will check for signs of cat flu.

• Drops or ointment may be prescribed. This may need to be administered up to four times a day to maintain the treatment at an effective level. Ointment should be gently applied over the eye surface, but be careful not to touch the eye with the nozzle. Wash your hands well after giving any treatment.

• With long-haired cats, excess hair can be trimmed from around the eyes.

• With an injury to the cornea, staining the surface of the cat's eye will enable the vet to assess the severity of the corneal ulcer. Most ulcers heal in 3–5 days with proper medication.

COMPLEMENTARY TREATMENTS

⊠HERBAL REMEDIES

Eyebright (*Euphrasia officinalis*) solution: 15 ml (1 tbsp) herb boiled then steeped in 300ml (half pint) water. Add 1.25 ml (1/4 tsp) sea salt. Strain. Apply to the eyes with cotton ball three times a day.

Alternatively, eyebright herb can be given as capsules one a day for four days.

Add garlic to the diet, one clove or capsule a day, plus a 250 mg supplement of vitamin C twice a day, for 14 days.

Make an eyebright rinse for conjunctivitis.

SNEEZING

Occasional sneezing is normal. It is a cat's way of clearing its nasal passages and need not be worrying. However, if the sneezing becomes frequent it may be a sign of an infection. A clear watery nasal discharge is often due to a virus or allergic component, whereas a thick, discoloured nasal discharge generally has a bacterial basis. If there is also loss of appetite and fever, take the cat to the vet.

CAUSES

• An infection of the upper respiratory tract is typically an early indicator of cat flu or similar illness. Feline viral rhinotracheitis (FVR) is more likely to result in sneezing than feline calici virus infection (FCV).

• Non-infectious causes may include a dusty environment, such as hay, or pollen from grass or wild flowers.

• If only one nostril is involved, it is possible that there is a cancerous growth in the nostril, especially in an older cat.

WHAT YOUR VET CAN DO

• The vet will identify whether the cause is infectious or non-infectious. In the case of a respiratory infection, antibiotics will help to reduce the severity of the illness, although they will not directly treat any viral infection.

• If a foreign body has triggered a fit of sneezing, the vet will give the cat an anaesthetic before examining the nose and extracting the offending object.

SYMPTOMS

• Constant sneezing.
• May paw at its nose.
• Depression.
• Possible fever.
• Loss of appetite.

Warning

Respiratory infections are easily spread from one cat to another by sneezing, as droplets travel through the air. Always keep a sick cat indoors to prevent the infection from spreading.

COMPLEMENTARY TREATMENTS

🗖 HOMEOPATHIC REMEDIES

Arsenicum album 30c, 1–2 drops by mouth once a day. Good for sniffles and thin nasal discharge. *Silica* 6c or 30c, once a day for 3 days, then 2–3 times a week to expel thick discharge and unblock nasal passages.

NASAL DISCHARGE

The link between the eyes and the nose means that, if the eyes are affected by cat flu, there is also likely to be a corresponding discharge from the nose. In the initial stages of a viral infection, the discharge will appear clear, becoming more mucus-like as the result of a secondary bacterial infection.

CAUSES

• Most often, a nasal discharge is the result of cat flu or other infection.

• Infection of the respiratory tract by mycoplasma organisms, which are midway between viruses and bacteria, will often be the cause of rhinitis, that is, inflammation of the nasal passages and a runny nose.

WHAT YOUR VET CAN DO

• The cat is likely to need a vitamin C supplement, continued for up to a month. You should keep it indoors and prevent contact with other pets while the discharge continues.

• Most nasal problems aren't serious and clear up well, but it is always best to check with your vet. There may be a secondary bacterial infection which may need antibiotic treatment to reduce the severity.

• Good nursing care is essential to help your cat recover. Providing lots of fluid is essential if the cat has become dehydrated. Hospitalization is likely to be needed in severe cases, especially as affected cats may lose their appetite.

SYMPTOMS

• Nose constantly running.
• Cat appears generally unwell.

Warning

Even after recovery, relapses may occur, particularly when the cat has been under stress of any kind, ranging from a spell in a cattery to a fight.

COMPLEMENTARY TREATMENTS

⊠ HERBAL REMEDIES

If the cat's nose has become sore by a constant discharge and subsequent rubbing, either almond oil or a calendula oil (see p. 11) gently applied to the affected areas can be very soothing.
For mild discharge, give 2 capsules *Echinacea* 10 days on, 10 days off.

▣ HOMEOPATHIC REMEDIES

Pulsatilla (anemone or windflower) 6c or 30c is frequently used to treat catarrh.

EAR PROBLEMS

A cat's ears are not only important for hearing, but are also vital for its balance. It is therefore important that your cat's ears are kept healthy and free from any parasitic infestation that, left untreated, can result in severe infections. Ear infection (otitis) can become chronic so, to reduce the risk of recurrences, a correct diagnosis of the cause is needed to decide treatment. Deafness can be hereditary, especially in the case of white cats. Old age can also result in some loss of hearing.

CAUSES

• Ear infections are most often caused by ear mites such as *Otodectes cynotis*, fungi or bacteria. Bacteria and yeast can occur together in an outer ear infection. The infection may extend from the outer ear through to the middle or inner parts of the ear if left untreated. An allergy may also give rise to a build up in the ear of a dark or yellowish waxy material.

• Microscopic mites commonly live in the ear canal and spread easily between cats and dogs. They make the ears itch so the cat will be constantly scratching.

• Blue-eyed white cats typically suffer congenital deafness because of malformation of the organ of Corti and associated structures within the ear. Deafness in the case of odd-eyed whites is confined to the side of the head corresponding to the blue eye.

• Occasionally, tumours occur in white-eared cats after repeated sunburn.

• In cases in which there has been recurrent irritation of the ear canal, polyps, which look rather like tumours, can develop.

• Swelling of the external ear flap (a haematoma) may derive from a bite or excessive head shaking.

SYMPTOMS

• Scratching the ears.
• Shaking of the head.
• Tilting the head.
• Discoloured material in one or both ears.
• Ear may be enlarged.

WHAT YOUR VET CAN DO

• In the case of an infection, the vet will examine the cat's ear with an otoscope. Mites will be clearly visible. The aural discharge can be cultured to ascertain the bacteria or fungi responsible so the necessary treatment can be prescribed for the mites and the infection.

• To treat mites, fungal or bacterial infestation, the vet will recommend a solution that can be squirted into the ear to clear the debris. The ear canal is then massaged for a few seconds and wiped out with a cotton ball. Two or three drops of medicine will then need to be applied to each ear daily for 7–10 days and massaged in.

• Nothing can be done for congenital deafness. Deaf cats should be kept indoors, well away from traffic.

• Tumours will require surgery. In the case of a haematoma, the swelling in the ear flap may have to be removed

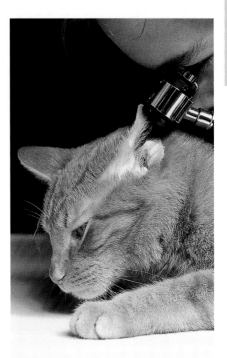

The otoscope can reveal the presence of mites or other problems in the cat's ears.

surgically by draining out the blood. The problem may recur. This type of fight injury is most commonly seen in unneutered tomcats, so neutering may also be advisable.

COMPLEMENTARY TREATMENTS

⬛ HERBAL REMEDIES

Calendula, 5 ml (1 tsp) in 250 ml (8 fl oz) of water, plus 2.5 ml (half tsp) of sea salt, can be used as an ear cleaner. Calendula oil can also be used to soothe red inflamed ears. Use 2 drops once a day and leave in ears.

To kill ear mites:
Yellow dock (*Rumex crispus*), 2 drops every third day for 3 to 6 weeks.

⬛ HOMEOPATHIC REMEDIES

Pulsatilla 6c, 1 pellet daily every third day for 30 days, can be used for painful ears. The cat will need to be held.

Sepia officinalis 30c, 2 whole or 3 crushed pellets twice a day, for 3 treatments. Can be beneficial for severe scratching and head shaking.

Calendula oil can relieve the pain of outer ear infections.

DENTAL HYGIENE

A cat's teeth are important for its overall state of health and your cat should be taken for an annual dental check-up. Cats are not prone to cavities, but dental hygiene is important to prevent the build-up of tartar, which can cause the gums to recede and teeth to become loose. Kittens do lose their baby teeth, so do not be surprised if your kitten has any loose milk teeth.

GOOD SIGNS

- Pink gums.
- White teeth.
- No trouble eating.
- No excessive salivation.
- No bad breath.

WHAT YOU AND YOUR VET CAN DO

• Ask your vet to show you how to clean your kitten's teeth properly. Begin when the cat is young, because it will be harder to persuade an older cat to let you touch its mouth. Start with a finger-stall rather than a brush and apply special toothpaste suitable for cats, which will not foam up in the mouth and upset your pet. You can brush with tuna juice, which works especially well with kittens. Introduce a brush later, taking care not to injure the gums. Brush each tooth surface for 30 seconds. There is no need to rinse the cat's mouth out after. You can brush its teeth daily or two or three times a week.

• Train your kitten to allow you to open its mouth soon after weaning, so that you will be able to clean its teeth (and also give tablets if need be). Hold the kitten's head across the bridge of the nose using your left hand (if you are right-handed), tilt the head upward and use your other hand to prise down the lower jaw.

• Good nutrition can help prevent bad breath, calculus build-up and inflammation of the gums (see p. 26). Vitamin supplements should be given to maintain strong teeth. To clear bad breath increase the stomach acid with acidophulus granules twice a week.

• Various foods will help to remove plaque and clean the teeth—crunchy brewer's yeast tablets or raw grated carrot.

COMPLEMENTARY TREATMENTS

⊠ HERBAL REMEDIES

Herbal toothpastes for cats contain sage oil, which not only cleans the teeth but also serves as a breath freshener. Alternatively, you can brush your cat's teeth with a weak salt and water solution.

Sage

DENTAL PROBLEMS

Dental care is important because 80 percent of cats over three years old have periodontal disease—that is, disease of the gums and tooth sockets. Furthermore, bacteria from tooth decay can lead to liver, kidney and heart disease. Any problems with the teeth or gums is likely to make it painful for your cat to eat.

CAUSES

• Lack of dental hygiene.

• Bacterial or viral infections, secondary to feline AIDS or leukaemia.

• Chronic disease of the kidneys or immune system can give rise to dental problems.

• Fights or car accidents can result in broken teeth.

BAD SIGNS

• Bad breath.
• Red, swollen gums.
• Cat salivates more than usual.
• Brown discoloured teeth.
• Gums bleeding.
• Cat has difficulty eating.

WHAT YOUR VET CAN DO

• If tartar is the problem, your vet will have to clean your cat's teeth, usually under anaesthetic with an ultrasonic descaler. In severe cases, a course of post-operative antibiotics may be prescribed to prevent infection. It will be up to you to encourage the cat to start eating again as soon as possible.

• Depending on the degree of damage, a tooth loosened in an accident may have to be removed.

• Abscesses will have to be treated with an antibiotic and possibly lanced, generally under anaesthetic.

COMPLEMENTARY TREATMENTS

HERBAL REMEDIES
A herbal solution to relieve inflamed gums and remove tartar: is a 60 ml (2 fl oz) of water, one-eighth tsp salt and 3 drops of tincture of myrrh. Wipe the gums once a day with a cotton swab.

Fragaria added to the diet after teeth cleaning will help prevent calculus build-up.

Goldenseal (Hydrastis canadensis) mouthwash can be used after dental cleaning. Stir 5 ml (1 tsp) of the powdered root into 600 ml (1 pint) of boiling water. Leave it to cool, then dab over the gums with cotton ball.

HOMEOPATHIC REMEDIES
Phosphorus, Sulphur or Silica can be used for long-term inflammation of the gums or mouth.

BAD BREATH

Bad breath, or halitosis, is a clear indication of disease of the teeth or gums. This is generally more common in older cats where plaque has built up on the teeth, fragments of food get trapped and gingivitis or inflammation of the gums results.

CAUSES

• The build-up of tartar or calculus on the teeth (see p. 19) is one of the most common causes of halitosis.

• In the case of long-haired cats, in particular, excessive salivation—often caused by tartar deposits—may mat the fur around the mouth, which then starts to smell unpleasant.

• When the cat grooms itself, loose hairs from the coat can become trapped between the teeth and start to rot.

• Chronic renal failure can also be responsible for giving the breath a sickly odour. If the breath smells sweet, this is an indication of diabetes (see p. 68). In both these cases, you should take your cat to the vet immediately.

WHAT YOUR VET CAN DO

• Your vet needs to determine the exact cause of the problem. Even if there are dental problems, there may be kidney failure as well, particularly in older cats. Cleaning the teeth will help get rid of tartar. Changing your cat's diet (see p. 72) can often help.

COMPLEMENTARY TREATMENTS

✠ HERBAL REMEDIES

After you have cleaned the cat's teeth, you can soothe the gums and help to prevent a recurrence by making an infusion of purple cone flower (*Echinacea angustifolia*). Put 5 ml (1 tsp) of rootstock and 250 ml (8 fl oz) of water in a saucepan. Cover and simmer the mixture for 10 minutes. Allow to cool for an hour, then strain. Wipe a little of the infusion over the cat's gums with a cotton ball. Repeat twice daily for about 10 days.

Note: This treatment is likely to promote salivation in the short term.

MOUTH ULCERS

There are two main causes of mouth ulcers. The most common is the calici virus which is part of the feline upper respiratory group of diseases (see p. 10). The ulcers, which make the cat drool, appear toward the end of the disease. The other cause of mouth ulcers, and sometimes those on the nose, roof of the mouth and tongue, is related to dysfunction of the immune system and stress in cats, generally female, about six years old.

CAUSES

• Major infection of the upper respiratory system, e.g. cat flu.

• Immune system problems in which stress is a predisposing factor causes what are called 'rodent ulcers', a misleading term that dates back to when it was thought the infection was contracted from mice or rats.

WHAT YOU OR YOUR VET CAN DO

• Your vet will prescribe antibiotics if there is secondary bacterial infection.

• You can enhance your cat's diet with raw liver, brewer's yeast, and vitamin supplements.

• If you purée the cat's meal and warm it a little, your pet will be manage to eat more of the food.

SYMPTOMS

• Red patches on tongue or gums.
• Cat has difficulty eating or stops altogether.

COMPLEMENTARY TREATMENTS

☐ **HOMEOPATHIC REMEDIES**
Kali bichromicum 200c may be given three times a week, for up to six weeks.

Natrum muriaticum is also used for oral problems including gingivitis, mouth ulcers and bad breath.

Potassium dichromate, the source of *Kali bichromicum*.

ASTHMA AND WHEEZING

Asthma is a disease of the respiratory system in which the immune system over-reacts to allergies or stress. Attacks are characterized by episodes of acute breathing difficulty and can be fatal if immediate relief is not available. It is becoming more common in cats as more of them spend their lives indoors and household allergens are increasing. The hay fever season often triggers sudden bouts of asthma or wheezing that spontaneously resolve themselves when the season ends. Your vet should ascertain the cause of any breathing difficulty.

CAUSES

• Inhaled allergens, such as pollen or mould outside.

• Household dust, house mites or household cleaning products indoors.

• Wasp or bee stings can trigger asthma attacks.

• Stress is a major cause of asthma.

• Lungworms reach the cat's lungs via the gut from the birds or frogs that the cat has caught and eaten. The cat tries to cough up the parasites which sounds like the dry cough of asthma.

SYMPTOMS

• Coughing (similar to hairball but often with difficulty breathing).
• Harsh whistling sound on intake of breath.
• Sudden respiratory distress.
• Mouth and tongue turn blue due to lack of oxygen.

THE RESPIRATORY SYSTEM

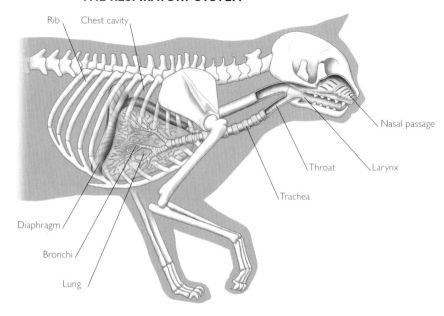

Rib   Chest cavity   Nasal passage   Throat   Larynx   Trachea   Diaphragm   Bronchi   Lung

WHAT YOU AND YOUR VET CAN DO

• The vet will do a physical exam, blood tests and possibly a chest X ray to pinpoint the exact cause of the breathing problem.

• If the cat is having serious breathing difficulty your vet may prescribe a bronchodilator, oxygen therapy or fast-acting steroids.

• At home, you can add antioxidant vitamins to the diet (vitamins C and E), which help to relieve asthma. You can also increase the fluids, such as tuna broth, and supplement the diet with raw meat, chopped greens, garlic and cooked vegetables.

• Increase the humidity in your home. Sit with the cat in a steamy bathroom for 30 minutes twice a day. Or use a vaporizer: add about 5 ml (1 tsp) of proprietary menthol or 3 drops of eucalyptus oil.

• Remove allergens from the environment: use dust-free unscented litter; get an air purifier and don't use scented carpet or lavatory sprays.

COMPLEMENTARY TREATMENTS

Acupuncture treatment can be very beneficial for cats with asthma.

Reduce infection by giving the cat garlic daily, a clove or a capsule added to food.

HOMEOPATHIC REMEDIES

For allergic reactions, *Rhus toxicodendron* Im (poison oak) may be beneficial. More localized infections can be treated with *Mercurius cyanatus* 30c (cyanate mercury). *Antimonium tartaricum* 30c (tartar emetic) can bring relief when the lungs are inflamed. Recovery from respiratory infections can be assisted by *Calcarea fluorica* 30c (calcium fluoride).

Garlic is a good natural remedy for chest infections.

SINUSITIS

Sinusitis is a rare condition in most cats, but it is more common in Siamese and similar oriental breeds. It is the result of chronic inflammation and infection of the nasal sinuses, the four air-containing cavities located in the face. If infection becomes trapped in these cavities, it can be painful for your cat, making breathing difficult. Persistent respiratory infections are quite common, particularly following cases of cat flu. Generalized signs of illness are likely to appear, such as loss of appetite and the appearance of the third eyelid, or haws, at the inner corner of the eye.

A cat with its haws visible.

CAUSES

- Potentially long-standing complication arising from cat flu.

- Infection by the fungal organism *Aspergillus*.

- Tooth abscess in the upper jaw.

- Long-term infection of bacterial or viral origin.

- Cancer of the nasal sinuses.

SYMPTOMS

- Discharge from the nose.
- Repeated sneezing.
- Loss of appetite.
- Appearance of the haws.

WHAT YOU AND YOUR VET CAN DO

- You can give saline nose drops—add 5 ml (1 tsp) of salt to 250 ml (8 fl oz) of water. Give 2–3 drops two or three times a day in each nostril to clear discharge. Another treatment is almond oil and vitamin E oil mixed in equal amounts—give 1 drop two or three times a day in each nostril.

- A more radical approach involves flushing the sinuses with an antibiotic fluid. If a tooth abscess has infected the sinus, the tooth will be removed.

COMPLEMENTARY TREATMENTS

□ HOMEOPATHIC REMEDIES

Lemna minor 6c (duckweed) is often recommended for the treatment of sinusitis.
In more stubborn cases, *Silicea* 200c (pure flint) can prove beneficial. This course of treatment will need to continue for a month.

Lemna minor

THE DIGESTIVE SYSTEM

Disturbances of the stomach and intestines in cats can be a result of a variety of things, including ingestion of bad food or foreign objects, infections, hairballs, parasites, allergies or diseases of different organs. The symptoms of digestive problems may include vomiting, diarrhoea or constipation. Most cats diagnosed quickly respond well to diet changes and medication. Long-term cases require more time and patience. A sick cat often stops eating, so monitoring its eating habits and general appearance should help you spot any health problems early on.

A HEALTHY DIET

Cats have very specific nutritional requirements, which must be met in their diet. Cats are true carnivores, that is, they must have meat and fish, which consist primarily of protein and fat, as the major ingredients in their diet. They cannot be kept on a vegetarian regime. They should have regular mealtimes, at least twice a day. In many cases, it is better to give smaller meals more often—it should be suited to the cat's age and lifestyle. Most owners prefer to offer a carefully balanced, complete diet rather than preparing fresh food for their pets. Good commercially available foods should have the contents clearly shown on the label along with the age group the food is suitable for.

2

YOUR CAT'S DIETARY REQUIREMENTS

• The most important factors in the day's eating are: 50–60 percent raw meat, 10–15 percent cooked vegetables, 10–15 percent cooked grains, 20 percent fresh greens, 10 percent fat.

• Essential amino acids are necessary to help a cat grow and stay healthy. Taurine is one which cats can't manufacture for themselves and it must come from animal protein in their diet. A deficiency can lead to blindness.

• Cats must have essential fatty acids, found in vegetable oils. Without them, a cat's coat loses its shine, and reproductive disorders may occur.

• A comprehensive range of vitamins and minerals needs to be present in your cat's diet. This is particularly true of vitamin A, since cats are unable to use carotenes to manufacture it.

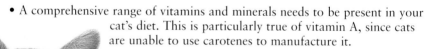

FEEDING TIPS

• Meals should be a specific amount left out for 20–30 minutes and then cleared away.

• Keep snacks to less than 5 percent of the total diet and make sure they are healthy ones.

• Offer different foods so that your cat learns to accept a variety.

• Don't give bones such as chicken to cats. They snap easily and can become lodged in the throat.

2

TYPES OF FOOD

Cat food can be divided into four basic categories:

• **Canned food** contains a high percentage of water, around 75 percent, which means that your cat will get enough fluid. It is less good for dental hygiene.

• **Dried food** has around 10 percent water. It is convenient, low-cost and good for dental hygiene. The main disadvantage is that it is not so tasty and not so easily digested.

• **Semi-moist food** contains around 35 percent water and costs mid-range beween wet and dry. The main disadvantage is that, once the sachet is opened, the food does not keep very long.

• **Fresh meat** has to be prepared by you. Most cats prefer this type, but it can be difficult to ensure your cat is getting the balance that is needed. Even prime steak is deficient in certain elements, for example it has a low calcium content. As an occasional treat, however, fresh meat, including raw liver, is fine.

AVOID:

• Overfeeding, which can lead to obesity.

• An exclusive diet of any one food.

• Milk, after the kitten stage, may provoke diarrhoea.

• Chocolate, which can cause seizures.

• Dog food, which is not suitable for cats.

Canned food

Dried food

Fresh food

VOMITING

A bout of occasional vomiting, for example bringing up hairballs, in an otherwise healthy cat is generally not a cause for concern. If it is persistent, however, with or without other signs of illness, appetite loss, depression or lethargy, diarrhoea or constipation, further investigation is needed by your vet so that the problem can be identified. Vomiting does cause dehydration so you should ensure that the cat has a plentiful supply of water.

SYMPTOMS

• Retching.
• Being sick.
• Appearing distressed.

CAUSES

• Eating grass or linear foreign bodies, e.g. string, rubber bands, or toys, or cat litter.
• Ingestion of poison.
• Renal failure.
• Parasites, that is, worms, especially in kittens.

WHAT YOU AND YOUR VET CAN DO

• Withhold food for 12–24 hours to allow the body to clear itself. Slowly reintroduce very small amounts of bland food, such as chicken baby food. If vomiting occurs again, call your vet. If the food stays down, gradually increase the amount. The diet should be back to normal in 3–5 days.

• If the cat has been poisoned, specific veterinary treatment is required immediately.

• Observe when the vomiting occurs and its appearance, so that you can give your vet a clear description.

• A cat that is vomiting due to chronic renal failure may require fluid replacement therapy by your vet (see p. 72).

COMPLEMENTARY TREATMENTS

⊠ HERBAL REMEDIES

After withholding food and water for 12–24 hours, try a little peppermint tea. If the cat does not vomit, move onto a little bland food.

⊡ HOMEOPATHIC REMEDIES

Arsenicum album 6c is useful to settle an upset stomach. Give every four hours; you should notice an improvement within a day.
Pulsatilla 6c is also good for treating nausea and vomiting if your cat has eaten fatty rich food.

HAIRBALLS

Hairball formation in cats is normal. The size of them and the number produced varies with the length of the haircoat, the amount of grooming activity, the season of the year—they are more common when your cat is moulting—as well as the general health and level of hydration of the cat. Most hairballs are vomited up without a problem but some can get very large and obstruct the intestines.

2

NATURAL PREVENTION

• Daily grooming eliminates extra hair, especially in long-haired cats.

• Observe whether the cat's grooming is excessive due to stress and try to eliminate the causes of stress (see p. 94).

• Feed a high-fibre diet, either natural with added chopped green vegetables or bran, or a commercially formulated diet.

• Add a regular laxative to the diet, such as 5 ml (1 tsp) of puréed prunes or one-eighth teaspoonful of slippery elm a day.

• Increase your pet's exercise with games or walks on the leash.

SYMPTOMS

• Reduced appetite.
• Occasional retching.
• Constipation.

WHAT YOU AND YOUR VET CAN DO

• If a large hairball forms, add a small spoonful of butter to the cat's food once a day for about five days.

• Your vet may have to operate to remove the obstruction from the cat's stomach, but this is usually the last resort after other means have failed.

COMPLEMENTARY TREATMENTS

☐ HOMEOPATHIC REMEDIES
Nux vomica (poison nut) is sometimes recommended for dislodging hairballs.

▨ DIETARY REMEDIES
Adding more fibre to your cat's diet can help to reduce the risk of a recurrence. Finely chop or grate a raw carrot and mix it well with canned food.

Alfalfa sprouts are also a good source of roughage. You can add a pinch to the cat's food daily. Both can help to restore the regular rhythm of the gut.

REFUSING FOOD

Cats are naturally finicky eaters and you should not worry if your pet refuses a meal occasionally. But, if it stops eating altogether for more than two days, you should consult your vet. The lack of digestive activity may promote hepatic lipidosis or fatty liver disease (see p. 70) in which fat accumulates in the cells of the liver. This causes further loss of appetite and thus perpetuates the illness.

CAUSES

• Noise can be a problem. Try offering the cat its food in a quieter corner, where it has the opportunity to feed undisturbed.

• Cats will often refuse to eat a different type of food that is unfamiliar to them. Some are even reluctant to switch brands of foods. Most problems are encountered when you are trying to change your cat from a wet diet (canned) to a dry diet.

SYMPTOMS

• Loss of interest in food over 2–3 days.

• Fright can put a cat off its food. Thunderstorms are a common reason for loss of appetite in the case of nervous cats.

• Impending or actual illness can make a cat lose its appetite.

WHAT YOU AND YOUR VET CAN DO

• You can try to stimulate your cat's appetite by warming its food slightly. Also try feeding it a smelly food such as fish. Spend time coaxing it, offering it food on your hand. The increased attention may stimulate its appetite.

• Your vet will try to ascertain the underlying cause of the lack of appetite.

• It may be necessary to rehydrate the cat with fluid injected sub-cutaneously.

• As a last resort, the vet may use a feeding-tube to make sure the cat gets some nourishment.

COMPLEMENTARY TREATMENTS

◪ DIETARY REMEDIES
It is sometimes possible to stimulate a cat's appetite with injections of vitamin B$_{12}$. Feeding a mixture of honey and yogurt may help, as can giving 125g (4 oz) raw liver once a week for life.

FELINE PERITONITIS

Feline Infectious Peritonitis (FIP) is caused by a virus infecting the stomach area but also affecting other adjacent organs. It is exacerbated by the cat's own immune system, which actually speeds the progress of the disease. FIP occurs in two forms: wet and dry. Cats of six months to two years old are the most susceptible although older cats can be infected. It is also more common in pure-bred cats and in cats living in a multi-cat environment. Once signs occur there is no effective treatment or cure. It is almost always fatal.

2

CAUSES

• FIP is caused by a virus which is transmitted in saliva, urine or faeces. The primary transmission is by mouth and nose. The virus lives up to seven weeks in the cat's surroundings but can be killed by bleach. The virus has a very variable incubation , The amount of time between the initial exposure to the virus and the outward signs can be several months to several years.

• Fifty percent of cats with FIP are also feline leukaemia positive.

• The affected cat must be isolated to attempt to prevent the spread of the disease to other animals.

SYMPTOMS

• Swollen abdomen.
• Fever and weight loss.

WHAT YOUR VET CAN DO

• There is no reliable blood test. The only effective diagnosis is by a tissue biopsy of the liver, but there may be signs of other diseases, such as leukaemia.

• A vaccine administered via the nose is available but is not of proven efficacy.

• There is no effective treatment. The immune system can be boosted, but mainly the only available care is to alleviate symptoms and ease discomfort.

COMPLEMENTARY TREATMENTS

🔲 HOMEOPATHIC REMEDIES
A nosode is available given at 16 weeks of age (see pp. 10–11).
Mercurius sulphuricus 6c, 1 pellet once a day for 30 days, can alleviate the fluid on the chest and difficult breathing.
Arsenicum album 6c, same dose as above, may help stress and anxiety.

🔳 BACH FLOWER REMEDIES
Rescue Remedy may be helpful to alleviate symptoms of distress.

Bach Rescue Remedy is bought ready mixed.

OBESITY

Twenty-five percent of cats are clinically obese, which means they are 15 percent over their ideal body weight. This is a serious condition because obesity reduces the cat's lifespan and makes it more likely to suffer from heart disease, diabetes, arthritis and lower urinary tract disease. Cats typically weigh between 2.7 kg (6 lb) and 8 kg (18 lb), depending on their ancestry. There should be a discernible waist with the chest wider than the abdomen. Cats store fat in the groin area so a bulge like an apple there is excess fat. Monitoring your cat's weight regularly is an important part of cat care as weight gain or loss is a significant indication that something is amiss. Helping a cat lose weight can be difficult; if it doesn't like what is served up it will go elsewhere to find other food to eat.

CAUSES

- Excessive food intake.

- Lack of exercise.

- Metabolic disorders.

SYMPTOMS

- Weight gain.
- Decreasing level of activity.

WHAT YOU AND YOUR VET CAN DO

- You should first check with your vet that the weight gain is not due to a systemic problem that can mimic obesity, such as hypothyroidism, heart disease, diabetes or liver disease.

- A diet for weight loss can be ready formulated, the key components being high protein and fibre, and low fat. Set a maximum initial weight loss at 15 percent and keep a chart of your cat's weight.

- Increase the number of meals to up to six a day. The more meals your cat eats, the more its metabolism is stimulated to burn calories.

- Do not feed table scraps and keep snacks to less than 5 percent of the diet. Try healthy treats like asparagus tips, carrots, unsalted popcorn or apple.

• Increasing the fibre in the diet provides bulk to fill the stomach.

• Try to persuade your cat to take some exercise—walks on a harness or games. Catnip may stimulate it to play. Aim at two 10-minute sessions a day.

• When the cat does reach its target ideal weight, change over to a commerical light diet and monitor its weight carefully over the next eight weeks. Continue to weigh your cat once a month for the first six months, then four times a year.

HOW TO WEIGH YOUR CAT

You may be able to persuade your cat to step on to the bathroom scales, but this may probably be impossible. It is easier if you pick up your pet and weigh both of you together. Then weigh yourself and subtract this figure from your combined weight.

WEIGHT GAIN AND NEUTERING

There are a number of advantages to having your cat neutered. In the case of queens, these include having no unwanted kittens, and in tomcats putting a stop to repeated fighting that can lead to injuries. However, the underlying hormonal changes will have an impact on your cat's metabolism, whatever its sex, so it is more likely to become obese. You will probably have to offer less food than you did before.

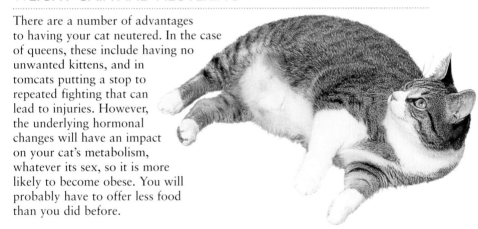

COMPLEMENTARY TREATMENTS

⊠ HERBAL REMEDIES
Adding 5 ml (1 tsp) of seaweed (kelp) powder to your cat's food may be beneficial if it has a slow metabolism.

Kelp powder

⊠ DIETARY REMEDIES
Cut out treats and try to bulk up your cat's rations by adding items of low calorific value, such as bran or finely grated or chopped carrot or apple, to the diet.

⊡ HOMEOPATHIC REMEDIES
Graphites be used to treat obesity as it helps the body to absorb nutrients.

DIARRHOEA

Diarrhoea can be a natural mechanism of the body to get rid of some foreign or toxic material that has been eaten. The cat will produce some loose or soft stools. However, if this becomes abnormally frequent, more liquid or lasts more than 24 hours you should take the cat to the vet. It may be a symptom of something more serious and will tend to lead to dehydration if not quickly treated.

CAUSES

• Bacterial or viral infection.

• Internal parasites, e.g. worms, especially in kittens.

• Food allergy—your cat may be allergic to milk, for example.

• Stress, changes in routine, or change of diet.

• Diarrhoea may be a symptom of a serious disease, especially of the liver or pancreas, or an immune-related disease, such as feline infectious peritonitis (see p. 31). This can lead to chronic diarrhoea, which will be fatal in kittens.

SYMPTOMS

• Loose faeces.
• Abdominal straining.
• Signs of abdominal pain.

HOME TREATMENT

• For simple diarrhoea, feed small amounts of bland, low-fat, easily digestible meals four times a day. Use lean protein, for example poultry, lamb or fish. Try the following diet:

Day 1: Withhold food for 12–24 hours, but make sure fluid is freely available to prevent the cat becoming dehydrated.
Day 2: Begin with small amounts of a bland food—chicken broth or puréed chicken baby food.
Day 3: Add in vegetables to increase fibre that absorbs liquid out the stool and firms it up.
Day 4: Add boiled white rice as a source of grain.
Day 5: Change from boiled white rice to boiled brown rice.
Day 6: Begin adding in some of the cat's normal diet, giving a quarter of the normal meal at a time, over three days.

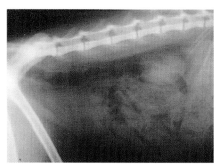

An X ray of your cat's stomach may be necessary to check for foreign bodies.

WHAT YOUR VET CAN DO

• Your vet will want to get a complete history of the problem and do a physical exam of the cat.

• The faeces will need to be checked for worms, which are especially common in kittens.

• If the cat is dehydrated, rehydration may be necessary. Rehydration can be by subcutaneous or intravenous injections.

• The vet may also carry out blood tests to rule out systemic disease or bacterial or viral infection.

• If you or your vet suspect that your cat may have swallowed something that is producing the diarrhoea, the vet may do an X ray or ultrasound scan. This will also reveal any cancerous growths.

Your cat is likely to be dehydrated after a bout of diarrhoea, so be sure to provide it with plenty of water.

COMPLEMENTARY TREATMENTS

HOMEOPATHIC REMEDIES
Natrium muriaticum 6x or *Podophyllum* 6c, 1 pellet every 4 hours for 3 treatments.

HERBAL REMEDIESS
Slippery Elm powder is a good treatment for diarrhoea. Put 5 ml (1 tsp) in 250 ml (8 fl oz) of cold water, bring to boil then simmer for 3 minutes. Allow to cool and give 2.5– 5 ml (half to 1 tsp) every 4 hours.

DIETARY REMEDIES
Live natural yogurt may have a beneficial effect, if your cat will try it.

Live natural yogurt

CONSTIPATION

Constipation is the inability to pass stools or the infrequent passage of stools that may be accompanied by signs of straining or discomfort. These symptoms too are part of feline lower urinary tract disease which is much more serious. As with constipation, the cat will make frequent trips to the litter box and strain. You should check the litter box for signs of urine as this disease can be fatal (see p. 74).

CAUSES

2

• Lack of fibre in the diet.

• Dehydration can precipitate constipation, because water is reabsorbed from the large intestine, making the passage of faecal material more difficult as a consequence.

• Dietary indiscretion, meaning that your cat has eaten something it should not have, cat litter or wool, for example.

• If a foreign body—usually a bone in the case of cats—becomes lodged in the intestinal tract, constipation may result. Chicken bones can be especially hazardous if they are swallowed.

• Hairballs may get caught in the intestine and cause constipation.

• Constipation can be a sign of certain disorders such as kidney disease, tumours, anal sac abscesses or a fracture in the pelvic region.

• Lack of exercise or obesity will cause a cat to be constipated.

SYMPTOMS

• Straining.
• Inability to pass a motion.

WHAT YOU AND YOUR VET CAN DO

• You can increase the fibre in the diet by adding fresh vegetables. In the long term, change the cat's diet to food with more than 10 percent fibre content. Include raw meat which acts as a natural laxative. Also provide more fluid. This can be either water, clam juice, fruit juice or, in this case, a little milk.

• If the stool is dry, a small spoonful of bran mixed into the meal twice a day helps the stool to retain moisture.

• Make sure the litter box is clean and fresh. The cat won't got to it and use it if it shows any signs of previous soiling.

• Try to increase the cat's exercise with games or walks. Groom the cat

2

regularly, especially if it is long-haired. Excess hair in the stool can cause constipation.

• Your vet will take a history of the problem, do a physical exam and obtain a faecal sample. A blood test may also be done to rule out kidney failure.

• The cat may need to be rehydrated, in serious cases by the vet at the practice.

• The vet may also do X rays to rule out tumours or fractures. The X ray will also show up cat litter or other foreign material in the intestine and how much material is backing up there.

COMPLEMENTARY TREATMENTS

⊠ HERBAL REMEDIES

Olive oil can lead to improved motility of the intestinal tract. Sprinkle 5 ml (1 tsp) over two of the day's meals to alleviate the situation.
Garlic also helps to prevent constipation, and most cats will eat it readily. Finely chop about half a clove and mix it in with the cat's usual food on a daily basis.

⊡ HOMEOPATHIC REMEDIES

In cases of severe constipation, the use of *Sepia* 30c can be helpful. It is made from the dried contents of the cuttlefish ink sac. Treatment may consist of a single dose.

FOOD ALLERGIES

Food allergy is an abnormal reaction to some ingredient in a food, quite frequently a protein source. About one third of allergic reactions in cats are thought to be of dietary origin, triggered, for example, by things such as cow's milk which a grown cat rarely needs. It is important to find out what the culprit is and remove it from the diet. Food allergies can be life-long and distressing if not dealt with.

2

CAUSE

• Common food allergens are beef, dairy products such as milk or cheese, eggs, fish, chicken, grains such as wheat and corn, tofu or even snacks or flavoured vitamins.

WHAT YOU CAN DO

An elimination diet is the only reliable method to identify the offending allergen:

• Begin with a totally new food. For example, if the cat has never had lamb, start with lamb baby food or puréed lamb chops. Feed it for a period of 12 weeks.

• Add previously given ingredients back into the diet one at time every 5–7 days until the problem recurs. You need to keep a note of what you did and when so you will then know which of the foods caused the reaction.

• Always use distilled water or boil tap water and refrigerate it.

• You could try a raw meat diet because raw meat does not cause the same allergic reaction as cooked meat.

• Once you identify the offending allergen you know what to look for on ingredient lists on bought meals.

SYMPTOMS

• Bladder infections, i.e. cystitis.
• Digestive problems, vomiting and/or diarrhoea.
• Itching can cause small scabs on the body that look similar to flea allergy.

COMPLEMENTARY TREATMENTS

☒ **HERBAL REMEDIES**
Vitamin C tablets may help to overcome symptoms of irritation, since at high doses this vitamin acts as a natural antihistamine, calming the body's response to an allergen. Giving 50 mg up to four times a day can be beneficial.

SKIN AND HAIR

The skin is the body's largest organ and acts as a protective barrier against cold, sunburn or infection. The condition of the skin and hair is a good indication of general health in a cat and if it is poor it usually indicates that something is wrong. This may be either a primary skin problem, such as fleas, or a secondary symptom of something more serious, for example in hyperthyroidism. A dull coat, flaky skin or a bad smell coming from the coat are all signs that should alert a cat owner. Most cats groom themselves regularly but if you also make a practice of grooming your pet this gives you the opportunity to see any change in its condition.

GOOD GROOMING

Grooming benefits your cat's health in many ways: it decreases hairballs and matted parts, removes dead skin and discourages fleas. Cats generally enjoy the activity, and it is a good way to reinforce the bond between you and your pet. Long-haired cats will soon get badly matted coats without your help. Older cats, especially if obese or arthritic, may need help to groom themselves. Generally, if a cat stops grooming itself, it is a sign of trouble.

3

Slicker brushes are particularly good for removing the dead hair on short-haired cats.

GROOMING TIPS

• Use the proper tools. Start with a comb, move on to a medium-soft brush or steel rake with widely-spaced blunt teeth.

• If your cat is reluctant to be groomed, try using a grooming glove which is coated with tiny plastic or rubber teeth. Your cat will think you are just petting it.

• How often you groom your cat depends on the length and type of coat and the cat's lifestyle, that is, whether it lives mostly inside or outdoors.

Slicker brush

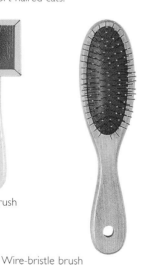

Wire-bristle brush

Nylon-bristle soft brush

Flea comb

• A cat's coat is either long or short, and single or double. Short-haired single-coated cats will only usually need grooming once a month. Use slicker brushes and groom them in the direction the fur is lying.

• Curly-coated cats, such as the American Wirehair and the Devon and Cornish Rex, should not be brushed or combed but given a monthly bath.

• Long-haired cats mainly need daily attention. You can groom them in different directions to prevent matting and remove as many loose hairs as possible. First brush the fur backward to raise it, then backcomb it. This approach is especially useful when it comes to removing the dense undercoat, which is less of a feature in the case of short-haired cats.

• Finish by combing the cat with a fine-toothed flea comb.

A wide-toothed comb is best for gently removing tangles from the coats of long-haired cats because it doesn't pull the fur.

3

BATHING YOUR CAT

• Prepare everything in advance, including the water, which should be tepid. Put a rubber mat on the bottom of the sink or large bowl to prevent slipping. Use a shampoo-spray device attached to the tap.

• Wear long sleeves and an apron and gloves to protect yourself from being soaked or scratched or bitten if your cat is nervous.

• Cut out matted bits in the coat first, as it is more difficult when the cat is wet, and trim its nails at this stage. Put cotton balls in the ears.

• You could put the cat in a harness and attach the leash to a suction plug on the wall to make the job easier. Gently wet the cat's coat, keeping the head dry if at all possible. Apply the prescribed shampoo.

• Rinse off the shampoo thoroughly, then wrap your cat in a towel and rub it dry. If your cat doesn't mind the noise, finish off with a hairdryer, on a low setting to avoid burning it. Do not let your cat out until its coat is fully dry.

ITCHING

Occasional itching, causing the cat to scratch itself briefly, is not a cause for concern. However, if your pet scratches repeatedly, especially in one particular area of the body, you need to establish the cause of the irritation, so that steps can be taken to deal with it before too much damage is done.

SYMPTOMS

- Repeated nibbling or scratching on one area of the body or generalized.
- Hair loss.
- Red bumps or pimples.
- Red and patchy, scabby skin.

CAUSES

- Allergic reactions, to pollen, dust or fleas.
- Bacterial infection is secondary to a primary problem such as fleas.
- Possible fungal problem, like ringworm.
- Dry skin.
- An insect bite.
- Parasite infestation, such as ear mites or lice.

WHAT YOU OR YOUR VET CAN DO

- You can bathe the cat in a hypo-allergenic shampoo or with bran (see Stud Tail p. 56).

- Moisturize the skin with 5 ml (1 tsp) of baby or mineral oil added to 5 litres (1 gallon) of water. Use as an after-bath rinse, or spray on (use a fine nozzle) a couple of times a week and leave to dry naturally.

- Dietary supplements: fatty acid supplements will clear itching and increase the shine of the coat. Good natural sources are fish, evening primrose, borage or safflower oils. Also give antioxidant supplements such as vitamin A and E.

- The vet will diagnose the underlying cause, possibly by examining a skin scrape under the microscope.

- Treatments prescribed may be steroids, antihistamines, anti-fungal drugs or dietary products.

3

Repeated scratching of the ears may indicate your cat has ear mites (see p. 17).

3

COMPLEMENTARY TREATMENTS

⊠ HERBAL REMEDIES

If one area is affected, trim any excess hair and bathe the so-called hot spot with a simple, non-medicated soap. Apply cold teabags to the site for a few minutes—the tannic acid which is present in tea aids the healing process. Aloe vera gel can also be soothing on the affected skin, or you can try yellow dock, burdock, nettles, cleavers or calendula to relieve the irritation.

Garlic can be included in the diet of a cat suffering from a flea bite allergy, to prevent further infestations. It can be given either fresh (finely chopped or grated) or as capsules.

⊡ HOMEOPATHIC REMEDIES

Graphites 6x is recommended when the affected areas are sore, and there is a thick discharge on the skin. This is normally given roughly every 4 hours, and an improvement should be discernible within a 24-hour period. If this does not work, a different remedy will be required.

Rhus toxicodendron 6x (poison ivy) should be used in the same way, for a maximum of five days. Stop the treatment earlier if the symptoms are alleviated. This is a more suitable remedy in cases of red, rather than broken, skin, particularly if there is also severe irritation.

More intense itching may respond better to *Arsenicum album* 30c (arsenic trioxide).

FLEAS

Fleas are the primary cause of itching in cats and one cat in four is allergic to flea saliva. The flea spends most of its time in the cat's surroundings, jumping onto your pet to get a feed and then jumping off again. But you can detect their presence by using a special fine-toothed flea comb—place the cat on a white sheet or paper. The black specks you comb out are actually flea faeces.

SYMPTOMS

- Scratching, particularly in neck and head area.
- Black specks in coat.

WHAT YOU AND YOUR VET CAN DO

- Give your cat a bath in shampoo which has pyrethrins or d-limolene as the active ingredient. These are natural flea repellants.

- Treat your home and all your pets at the same time—fleas will bite animals and people (you will find tell-tale bumps on your lower legs). The best home treatment (once a year) to protect you and your pets is borax powder, sprinkled on the carpet and upholstery, then vacuumed up. Remember to remove and throw the vacuum bag in the garbage bin.

- Powders, sprays and shampoos are traditional methods of control, but it is important to ensure you use them strictly in accordance with the instructions, to safeguard your cat's health. Flea collars are not considered effective and can cause skin allergy.

- Generally, you can deal with fleas without your vet but many insect growth regulator (IGR) products are only available on veterinary prescription. This treatment blocks the development of the flea's life cycle, preventing their eggs from hatching successfully. They are sprinkled over the cat's food, or given by injection.

COMPLEMENTARY TREATMENTS

✠ HERBAL REMEDIES
A herbal flea dip can be made from 5 ml (1 tsp) dried rosemary, or 15 ml (1 tbsp) fresh, in 600 ml (1 pint) of boiling water. Steep for 10 mins, strain, leave to cool before using.

A natural treatment for the outdoor environment are nematodes, microscopic worms which eat harmful insects. They can be obtained from pet or garden stores and are sprayed on the garden.

FLEA BITE ALLERGY

Fleas feed by penetrating the cat's skin with their sharp mouthparts, injecting saliva and then sucking up the resulting cocktail. Some cats can become allergic to saliva left in the skin and may develop severe signs of irritation. The likelihood of an allergy developing is greater in cats that have been regularly exposed to fleas, so effective flea control is essential. This reduces the risk of exposure and the subsequent skin problems associated with an allergy.

SYMPTOMS

- Hair loss.
- Secondary bacterial infection.
- Intense irritation.
- Small swellings may spread over the body.

CAUSE

- Once your cat has become sensitized to fleas' saliva, the presence of even a single flea on its body can result in a severe allergic reaction.

WHAT YOUR VET CAN DO

- Treatment to overcome the dermatitis, that is inflammation of the spots under the fur, may initially involve administering a short-acting corticosteroid to relieve the worst of this irritation.

- Because fleas suck blood, the vet may recommend vitamin B and iron, especially for kittens as they are prone to anaemia. Brewer's yeast is a good source and easy to give in food.

- A flea-control method based on an IGR (insect growth regulator) will provide long-term protection for your cat and your home.

3

COMPLEMENTARY TREATMENTS

⊠ **HERBAL REMEDIES**
Bathe the affected area with diluted lemon juice to soothe it and lessen the risk of a secondary infection developing. Wash and slice an organic lemon and add it to 600 ml (1 pint) of warm water. Leave to steep overnight, then strain out any fibrous pieces. Using cotton balls, gently apply this solution to the cat's skin.

A natural herbal itch remedy is cats claw (*Acacia greggi*) and dandelion. Mix 5 drops of each, give three drops of the mixture once daily, for 14 days, into the mouth, in food or in water.

As well as being anti-inflammatory, lemon also acts as an antihistamine.

TICKS

Ticks are most often encountered in agricultural areas, where sheep and cattle are their usual hosts. These parasites have a complex life cycle. The eggs hatch into larvae that, along with the next stage in their life cycle, called nymphs, attach themselves to farm livestock. They then drop off their hosts to mature and wait in turn for another animal, such as your cat, to pass by. Once the tick, which is the size of a pinhead, has managed to gain a grip on the cat's body, it will start to feed, piercing the skin with its sharp mouthparts. As the tick sucks the cat's blood, it swells significantly in size, and can grow to the size of a small fingernail. It is most likely to be seen at this stage, usually when the cat is being stroked or groomed.

Tick

3

SYMPTOMS

• The way in which the tick is embedded in the skin may make you think that it is a wart or a swelling. On closer examination, however, you will be able to see the legs and mouthparts. The coloration can vary, depending on the type of tick.
• Cat will scratch at the area.
• Secondary infections of the skin may develop.
• Blood parasites may be transmitted to the cat by the tick.

WHAT YOU CAN DO

• Although it may be tempting to try to pull the tick out of the skin, don't do it. You will simply detach the tick's body, leaving its head and mouthparts embedded in the skin, where they are then more likely to result in an infection. You can buy a spray that causes a tick to loosen its grip, but the simplest solution is to coat the parasite with petroleum jelly, particularly towards its rear. This should block the tick's breathing tube, so it suffocates and detaches quite rapidly of its own accord. Alternatively, you can dab alcohol on the tick to kill it.

• If your cat is heavily infested, then a commercial insecticide may be necessary. You should consult your vet on the best treatment.

COMPLEMENTARY TREATMENTS

⊠ HERBAL REMEDIES
Dab the site of attachment with calendula cream to promote healing and lessen the risk of infection.

Calendula comes from marigold flowers

LICE

There are two types of lice: those that bite and those that feed by sucking blood. Only the biting ones have been recorded in cats and they are known to cause anaemia if the animal is run down. They are rarely found on healthy, domestic cats. Lice are visible to the naked eye under a bright light but the tiny white nits—which are the egg cases—may be more visible attached to the hair of the coat. Lice only occur in the cold winter months and do not infest the home.

SYMPTOMS

- Irritation and itching.
- Rough, damaged coat.
- General ill-health, especially in kittens.
- Possible anaemia.

CAUSES

• Lice are most likely to appear in cats kept in close proximity to each other. It is always worthwhile checking the fur and skin carefully if your cat has come from a rescue home, or has spent some time in a cattery.

• Kittens are particularly vulnerable to lice, especially if they are suffering from malnutrition or are weak. If one kitten in a litter has lice, all are likely to be infested.

3

WHAT YOU AND YOUR VET CAN DO

• Grooming can help to control lice, because they die quickly when removed from contact with the cat.

• Treatment is the same as for fleas (see p. 44). Most products that kill fleas will kill lice. A second application of insecticide is necessary after a fortnight or so to destroy lice that have hatched from eggs in the meantime.

• Bathe your cat with a pyrethrum shampoo once a week for three weeks, leaving the suds on for 10 minutes before rinsing off. Repeat as above.

• Your vet may recommend an antihistamine to control the itching and advise on giving dietary supplements with B vitamins and iron—for example, brewer's yeast or raw liver—to combat possible anaemia.

COMPLEMENTARY TREATMENTS

⊠ HERBAL REMEDIES
Citrus-based shampoos, which contain the natural insecticide d-limolene, can be used to control lice.

◪ DIETARY REMEDIES
Especially with kittens, brewer's yeast

tonic, which is rich in vitamin B, can help combat the anaemia that may result from lice or other parasitic infestation.
    Alternatively, add foods rich in vitamin B, such as liver and eggs, to the cat's diet.

MANGE

Parasitic microscopic mites cause this disease. The form known as sarcoptic mange is the type most likely to affect cats. Mites burrow into the skin, laying their eggs. This causes an infection that spreads easily, with signs becoming evident anywhere from two weeks to two months after the cat was first exposed. Mites spread either by direct contact between cats (or dogs) or indirectly by means of contaminated grooming tools. They can infect people as well, causing scabies—all family members may have to be treated to eliminate the parasite. Demodex mites, by contrast, invade the cat's hair follicles and sometimes the sweat glands. They are usually spread from a queen to her kittens, with the symptoms becoming apparent later in life.

A mange mite

SYMPTOMS

Sarcoptic mange
• Tips of the ears often affected first,
• Skin becomes dry and crusty,
• Area is very itchy.

Demodectic mange
• Hair loss,
• Affected area grows in size,
• Skin may become red and inflamed with pus-filled spots.

CAUSE

• Mite infestation.

WHAT YOUR VET CAN DO

• Your vet will examine skin samples under the microscope to identify the mites. Scrapings from several affected areas may be required to detect sarcoptic mites, while demodex mites have to be squeezed out of the follicles to be seen.

• Treatment of sarcoptic mange invariably proves to be easier than that of demodectic mange. For sarcoptic mange, the hair will have to be clipped over the affected areas and the skin washed with a special shampoo before actual treatment is applied. This treatment will need to be repeated over a few weeks in order to eliminate the mites. If your cat has mange of this type, always make sure you wear gloves when treating or grooming your pet, and children should be told to wash their hands after any contact with it.

• Demodex mange can sometimes heal spontaneously if it is localized, but more often the mites spread rapidly over the cat's body. This is why early diagnosis and treatment are very important, especially as bacteria can invade the affected areas, causing a serious and even life-threatening secondary infection needing antibiotics.

Warning

Be sure to wash or replace all bedding regularly to reduce the risk of your cat becoming reinfected. Grooming tools may also spread the infection. If you have more than one cat, or a dog, watch for signs of mange in them. You should seek veterinary advice for this condition.

• It will be helpful to boost your cat's immune system, as this increases the likelihood of the infestation curing itself spontaneously. Provide supplements for this purpose, notably zinc and vitamins C and E. Although this combination is found in most general purpose preparations, it may be better to provide them individually. Your vet will be able to advise you about dosages, which depend partly on the size of your cat. A supplement of essential fatty acids may also be recommended.

COMPLEMENTARY TREATMENTS

▣ HOMEOPATHIC REMEDIES

Sulphur 6x may be used on a daily basis for a month. It is likely you will need to reduce the frequency of treatment as the symptoms disappear.

✕ HERBAL REMEDIES

Soothe the affected areas by washing them each day using a lemon juice solution (see p. 45). This may help to kill some of the mites.

Lavender oil, diluted 1:10 with almond oil, may help to encourage new hair growth in the case of demodectic mange. Apply daily to the skin until the new hair starts to appear. Purple coneflower (*Echinacea angustifolia*) can be used for sarcoptic mange. Apply recommended solution of the tincture over the affected area.

Purple coneflower

RINGWORM

In spite of its name, this is actually a fungal infection rather than a parasitic disease. It can be transmitted from animals to people and, in fact, the first indication of the disease may not come from your cat, as the symptoms may show up more clearly in you or another member of the family. The forearms are a common site for the red circular patches that characterize human cases of ringworm. It most commonly affects kittens or young cats under a year old.

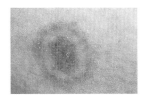

Human ringworm

SYMPTOMS

- Circular areas of hair loss, especially on head, ears, paws and back.
- Edges of areas may be red and scaly.
- Some itching.

3

CAUSES

- A range of fungi.

WHAT YOU AND YOUR VET CAN DO

- Your vet can examine your cat under an ultraviolet Wood's lamp to diagnose ringworm as some of the fungi that cause it, though not all, become fluorescent under UV light.

- Skin cultures can also be set up to identify the fungus. It can take two or more weeks to obtain a definite result.

- You can trim the hair round the bald spots using an electric clipper to help prevent spread. The infection is at its most active in the outer part of the affected area, in both people and cats. Remove and sterilize the clipper blades after use. (When treating your pet, stand it newspaper which can be quickly wrapped and discarded.)

- Washing the bald spots once a day with iodine or a chlorhexidine type of soap will help to prevent secondary infection.

- Treatment may include applying topical antifungal creams, such as ketaconazole, as directed, using disposable gloves.Griseofulvin tablets may be prescribed for severe cases, but these are not suitable for pregnant cats.

A ringworm lesion is visible above this kitten's right eye.

• Try to keep the infected cat away from other household pets (and children).

• Cat flaps can hinder treatment and spread the condition in a household with many cats. As the cats brush against the frame when they come in and out, they contaminate the sides. You can try cleaning the area with an anti-fungal spray.

3

Warning

The main aim is to stop the infection being transmitted to other members of the household, including other pets. Dogs are susceptible to the same strains as cats, so it is advisable to have them screened by the vet, along with any other cats. The fungal spores which cause ringworm survive well on bedding and carpeting so regular washing and cleaning is essential.

COMPLEMENTARY TREATMENTS

⊠ HERBAL REMEDIES
Goldenseal (*Hydrastis canadensis*) can be infused by stirring a generous 5 ml (1 tsp) of powdered rootstock into 250 ml (8 fl oz) boiling water. When this has cooled, strain the fluid into a separate container. Use to massage the affected area morning and evening (wear gloves). Plantain leaves (*Plantago major*) can be infused in the same way and used to wash the lesions.

☐ HOMEOPATHIC REMEDIES
Sulphur 6x, 1 tablet once a day for 30 days, can be used with one of the herbs above.

Golden seal

DANDRUFF

The skin is the largest organ of the body, accounting for nearly a quarter of a cat's weight in the case of young cats. A degree of skin loss is quite normal in all cats—the outer layer of the epidermis, called the stratum corneum, is shed and replaced by new growth from beneath continuously. This can become extreme however, and, as the skin gets drier, small flakes of dandruff become apparent. Looking almost the same on a cat are Cheyletiella mites which are a parasitic infestation known as 'walking dandruff'.

Brushing, rather than combing your cat, can help to remove any skin flakes..

3

SYMPTOMS

• Flakes of skin are shed through the hairs.
• Flakes show up on the brush or comb during grooming.
• If mites are the cause they appear as flakes as the cat scratches.

CAUSES

• Drying out of skin.

• Anything that causes irritation to the skin, such as external parasites, an allergic reaction or an infection may lead to dandruff. Your vet try will distinguish between these various possibilities.

WHAT YOU AND YOUR VET CAN DO

• Brushing will remove the shed flakes of skin. Washing with a mild oatmeal-based shampoo may help to soothe the skin.

• Follow the directions for dry skin opposite.

Dandruff in a cat's coat.

COMPLEMENTARY TREATMENTS

◪ DIETARY REMEDIES
Dandruff caused by dry skin is linked to a shortage of dietary fat, so adding a small spoonful of corn oil to your cat's food each day can be beneficial.

Corn oil is beneficial for dry skin conditions.

DRY SKIN

Both external and internal factors may contribute towards skin dryness. Repeated use of flea shampoos, for example, tends to dry the skin, leading to flaking as well. Mites which cause 'walking dandruff' affect the skin. A sluggish thyroid gland (see p. 68) may have a direct influence on the state of the skin, and is often accompanied by other symptoms, hair loss being the most obvious. It is therefore important for your vet to determine whether the cause of dry skin in your pet is primary or secondary, that is, the result of a disorder present in another organ of the body.

CAUSES

- Shampoo used for flea control.
- Mites of the Cheyletiella type.
- Endocrine disturbance.

SYMPTOMS

- Dry, sometimes crusty skin.

WHAT YOU AND YOUR VET CAN DO

3

- It may help to use a humidifier in your home or place bowls of water by the radiators to keep the air moist.

- You can bathe the cat using a moisturizing shampoo once a month.

- Your vet will examine the cat, and may do blood tests, to identify the exact cause of the condition so the right treatment can be prescribed. If there is mite infestation, there may be crusty areas of dry skin, often roughly circular in shape, forming over the cat's neck and body. Cases of this infestation are not common, but care needs to be taken because the mites can be spread to people, most commonly when affected cats are allowed to sleep on the bed. Your vet will probably recommend an insecticidal compound, often in the form of a wash, which needs to be applied to the parts of the body where the cat scratches.

COMPLEMENTARY TREATMENTS

⊠ HERBAL REMEDIES
Washing the affected areas with lemon water (see p. 45) can help, because of the presence of a natural insecticidal compound in the juice.

▣ HOMEOPATHIC REMEDIES
Sulphur 6x, taken every second day for a month, may be recommended. You should see signs of improvement within the month.

HAIR LOSS

Cats can lose clumps of hair as a result of fighting or through stress. However, it is more commonly the result of a skin complaint, such as dermatitis when an area of skin becomes inflamed. It may also be an outward sign of an underlying illness, but in this case the cat will generally be quite ill by the time the coat begins to deteriorate. Cats also shed their hair seasonally, depending on the breed, but this shedding, or moulting as it is known, is more irritating than dramatic.

3

CAUSES

• Hair loss can occur when the cat is suffering from some kind of skin condition, brought on either by an allergy or by a parasite or mite infestation which causes itching. In these cases, the skin which is revealed by the absence of hair in the area will not look healthy.

• In the case of dermatitis brought on by a flea bite allergy (see p. 45), the skin will be reddened and covered in scabs where the cat has been scratching itself.

• If it is a manifestation of illness, and sometimes poisoning, the affected areas may be localized or extend over much of the cat's body.

• Hormonal imbalance can trigger hair loss.

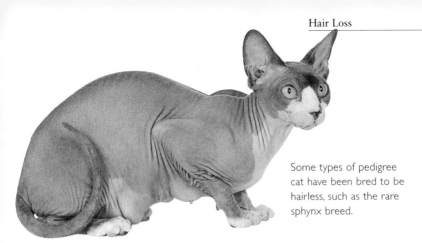

Some types of pedigree cat have been bred to be hairless, such as the rare sphynx breed.

• Female cats sometimes suffer temporary loss of hair soon after giving birth.

• If you notice that the loss of hair is affecting both sides of the body in a symmetrical way, this is almost certainly indicative of an endocrine disorder.

• Seasonal thinning of the hair is quite natural, especially in the case of long-haired breeds such as the Norwegian forest cat. This particular breed loses much of its distinctive facial ruff in the spring, when the weather becomes warmer.

3

WHAT YOUR VET CAN DO

• Hair loss due to mites or any other parasite may need veterinary attention. A safe insecticide treatment will be prescribed for mange. Ringworm (see p. 50) can be treated using anti-fungal cream prescribed by your vet. More severe cases may require anti-fungal drugs.

• If the fur loss is caused by an endocrine disorder, a series of tests should be carried out by your vet, to ascertain its exact nature. Only in this way can the most suitable course of treatment be prescribed.

COMPLEMENTARY TREATMENTS

⊠ HERBAL REMEDIES
Kelp powder—about 5 ml (1 tsp) daily —sprinkled over the cat's food can help to boost a sluggish thyroid gland.

▢ HOMEOPATHIC REMEDIES
Thuya occidentalis 30c, derived from fresh twigs, can be helpful. Three doses given 12 hours apart are normally recommended. If this fails, then *Selenium* 30c may be prescribed. Hair loss in queens after giving birth can be corrected by raising the protein level of their diet and dosing once with *Sepia* 30c.

STUD TAIL

This is a localized infection of the base of the tail that can afflict cats of either sex, whether neutered or not, but is most common in unneutered males. It is also particularly common with curly-coated rex breeds, the Devon and Cornish Rex.

SYMPTOMS

- Grease accumulates on the fur, matting it and causing it to take on a crusty appearance.
- The area may become infected.

CAUSE

- Overactive secretion from the sebaceous glands on the upper surface of the tail possibly due to hormonal activity.

WHAT YOU AND YOUR VET CAN DO

- The treatment is the same as for feline acne (see opposite page). You can bathe the affected area using a mild baby shampoo to break down the grease. Do not be tempted to use a medicated shampoo, because this can dry out the skin and ultimately worsen the condition. Alternatively, you can give the cat a bran bath to save you having to wash the affected area repeatedly. This keeps the coat in general free from grease and is less stressful for the cat.

HOW TO GIVE A BRAN BATH

The bran, which acts as a dry shampoo, can be bought from most pet shops. Warm it on a tray in the oven, and then tip it into a bowl. Place an old sheet or newspaper on top of a table, or where the mess you'll be making won't be a problem. Hold your cat and massage the bran thoroughly into its coat, as close to the skin as possible. Although messy, this is far less upsetting for your cat than washing its coat with shampoo and water. After a while, brush the bran, which will have absorbed the grease, out of the fur and throw it away.

Gently rub the bran into the fur.

Brush out the bran with a soft-bristled brush.

ACNE

Acne is a localized bacterial inflammation of the skin associated with overactive and possibly blocked glands. It can strike cats of any age. Rapid treatment at the outset is recommended. Some vets think it may be linked in some way with stress or hormonal activity.

CAUSES

• Infection enters area of skin where sebaceous glands are blocked. Repeated scratching exacerbates the problem.

SYMPTOMS

• Inflamed and infected skin under jaw.
• Pimples may appear.

WHAT YOU AND YOUR VET CAN DO

• Try encouraging the blocked glands to open by holding a warm cloth to the area for 3–5 minutes twice a day.

• Clean the area with an anti-bacterial solution, such as iodine or chlorhexidine. Rinse with water, then blot with alcohol or hydrogen peroxide to dry it out.

3

• Do not use human acne treatments, as these could prove harmful to your cat. Do not squeeze the spots, because this may spread the infection or increase the amount of time it takes for the acne to heal.

• Some vets think acne is caused by a reaction to plastic so you can try changing your pet's bowls to metal or pottery.

• Your vet may decide to treat the infection with antibiotics.

COMPLEMENTARY TREATMENTS

⊠ HERBAL REMEDIES
Aloe vera gel will soothe and help to heal the affected area.
Calendula tincture, six drops in 30 ml (1 fl oz) water. Dab on area twice daily with a cotton ball (discard after use). This speeds healing and helps clear up bacterial infections.

Aloe vera

SUNBURN

Although the idea of cats getting sunburn may seem strange, it does in fact happen, partly because of cats' natural behaviour. They will often seek a sunny spot and lie there for long periods, seemingly oblivious to the heat. Even in a temperate climate, on a warm summer's day a cat can be burned by the sun. White cats and cats with sparse fur are the most susceptible. Repeated exposure may lead to the development of cancer, especially on the tips of the ears.

3

SYMPTOMS

• Reddened areas on parts of the body where the skin is directly exposed to the sun's rays, particularly on the edges and tips of the ears and the nose. If the cat has been sleeping on its back, the underparts may also be burned, as the covering of fur is relatively thin there.

• Cat will rub or lick the affected areas.

CAUSE

• Overexposure to sunlight.

WHAT YOU CAN DO

• Always try to prevent your cat from getting sunburned, rather than having to treat it. You may need to alter your own routine, by placing your pet outdoors early in the morning before the sun is at its hottest, for example, and then luring it back indoors before midday when the sun is directly overhead. Do this by providing some food in the late morning and then keep your cat inside until well into the afternoon. A cat is usually just as happy sleeping in its bed over this period, rather than outside.

• In hot weather, use a sunscreen on vulnerable parts of the body. Specially formulated products for this purpose are available in many pet shops. Do not use sunscreens made for people, since they contain potentially harmful ingredients, notably zinc oxide and PABA (para-aminobenzoic acid), which cats will ingest when they lick their fur. Use a sunscreen with a Sun Protection Factor (SPF) of over 30. When applying, try to rub it in as much as possible, so that it has a chance to be effective, rather than licked off.

• Distracting your cat for a time by playing with it will give the skin a chance to absorb the cream.

3

• You may have to consider protective clothing for the cat's vulnerable areas.

• If your cat becomes sunburned, it is important to provide relief without delay. The affected areas will be red and inflamed, as well as very tender, so handle the cat with particular care. The best way to cool the skin is by gently covering it with a flannel soaked in cold or tepid water. Don't let it dry out. Repeat every 30 minutes or so for a period of between two and three hours.

COMPLEMENTARY TREATMENTS

✠ HERBAL REMEDIES

Applying witch hazel (*Hamamelis virginiana*) lotion can provide relief, and helps the healing process. Use about every four hours.

Aloe vera—taken directly from the plant or purchased in gel form—smeared over the sore area should be soothing and healing.

Witch hazel

CLAWS

Cats depend on their claws for a variety of tasks, including grooming, catching prey and climbing. The surgery known as declawing, in which the claws are removed, is cruel and interferes with the cat's natural pattern of behaviour. It is prohibited in a number of countries. Conflict arises in the home if the cat decides to use a piece of furniture for sharpening its claws, a particular problem for cats that live permanently indoors. The simplest solution is to buy a scratching post and train your cat to exercise its claws here. Start by gently rubbing the front paws down the post to give the cat the idea.

3

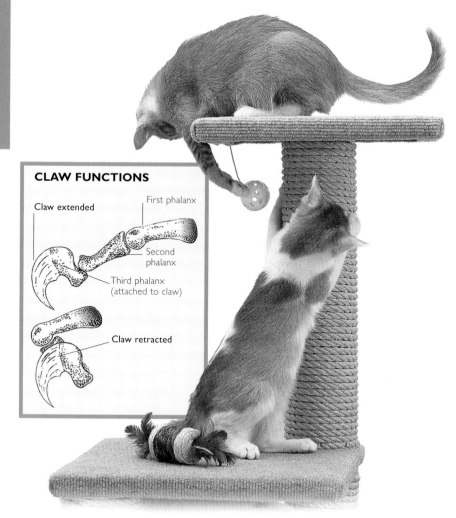

CLAW FUNCTIONS

Claw extended

First phalanx

Second phalanx

Third phalanx (attached to claw)

Claw retracted

SCRATCHING ISSUES

• As well as keeping the claws short, scratching plays an important role in territorial marking, which is one reason cats instinctively return to the same spot. It provides a visual sign to other cats in the neighbourhood of your cat's presence, making up for the loss of scents, which are likely to be diluted during heavy rain. When scratching to mark its territory, the cat also leaves behind a scent, from sweat glands located between the toes. Once you have encouraged your cat to use a scratching post in the home, therefore, it will be drawn back to the same spot because of its scent.

• If you find that your cat is starting to scratch furniture, a simple scolding may not be enough. You need to wipe over the area with water or something stronger like cologne to remove the cat's scent (see Chapter 5 for more information about behavioural training).

• Less agile older cats will scratch less and the claws may have become overgrown, so that the cat may have difficulty when walking, especially on carpet. If your pet's claws get caught up in the fibres, the tips of the claws may need clipping back. If the tips of the claws stick out when you lift the paw instead of being retracted. then clipping will be necessary.

WHAT YOU AND YOUR VET CAN DO

3

• If you are in any doubt about whether your cat's claws need clipping, arrange to see your vet, who will also be able to carry out this task for you. Clipping must be carried out in a good light using a special pair of clippers. Avoid cutting the nail too short or splitting it, both of which will be painful and distressing for your pet. The blood supply extends down from the base of the claw as a thin pink streak. Make the cut further down the claw, below the streak, so that bleeding does not occur.

• Sometimes, particularly if they are overgrown, the claws may become torn. This can lead to more serious injury that will require veterinary attention. In some cases, the claw may have to be removed by your vet. The affected area should be kept bandaged for a while, until healing has begun. This will reduce the likelihood of an infection developing.

If you are unsure of how to clip your cat's claws, ask your vet to show you.

ABSCESSES

Abscesses are pockets of pus under the skin. Pus is an accumulation of bacteria and white blood cells and indicates the presence of infection. Abscesses occur most frequently in unneutered tomcats that get bitten as they compete for territory. Bacteria from the rival cat's mouth enter the puncture wounds in the cat's skin. The problem is detection: because cat fur is so dense, it may not be immediately apparent that it has been bitten but eventually a lump forms. On occasions the abscess may burst of its own accord.

SYMPTOMS

- The fur may be damp from the other cat's saliva and you will be able to discern toothmarks.
- Once the bacteria start to multiply in the wound, a lump will form quickly.
- The resulting swelling feels hot to the touch and continues to increase in size until it is ready to burst.
- By this stage, your cat is likely to be acting generally off-colour, and suffering loss of appetite as well.

CAUSES

- Abscesses generally result from a bite by another cat, frequently on the side of the face, although they can occur virtually anywhere on the body. The cat's sharp, pointed canine teeth located at the corners of the mouth act like needles, injecting bacteria deep into the wound.

Unneutered cats are more likely to get involved in territorial disputes with neighbouring cats.

WHAT YOU AND YOUR VET CAN DO

• Soak the area of the bite in a solution of Epsom salts, which may help to bring the abscess to a head. Once the abscess reaches this stage, you should take the cat to the vet.

• Try giving your cat 250 mg vitamin C tablets three times daily, for three days, when the abscess becomes apparent. This vitamin boosts the cat's immune system.

• Once the abscess has formed, the vet will lance and drain it, then prescribe antibiotics to kill the bacteria and prevent any further infection.

• Unless your cat is used for breeding it is worth considering having it neutered. After neutering, cats become less territorial and less likely to fight.

3

COMPLEMENTARY TREATMENTS

⊠ HERBAL REMEDIES

Once the abscess has burst, a tincture of calendula, made by stirring 1.25 ml (1/4 tsp) of calendula oil into 250 ml (8 fl oz) of warm (not boiling) water, will assist the healing process. Apply twice daily.

⊡ HOMEOPATHIC REMEDIES

Ledum (marsh tea), with a recommended potency between 6c and 200c, is frequently used for treating abscesses. This treatment can be combined with *Hypericum* as well, but you will need to consult a homeopathic vet for specific dosages.

When it appears ready to rupture, *Hepar sulphuris*, starting with a potency of 6c, is often beneficial. The dosage is normally increased to 200c during the healing phase. Keep wiping the area with damp cotton balls, to allow the pus to drain out of the tooth holes properly. *Silicea* 200c can be helpful in assisting the cat's general recovery.

CUTS AND STINGS

There are many everyday hazards that cats face, ranging from insect stings to broken pieces of glass. If your cat is inclined to investigate the contents of rubbish bags it is likely to be cut, or stung by wasps buzzing round the waste. Kittens are especially vulnerable to suffer stings, being naturally curious and unaware of the hazards of snapping at flying insects. Having been stung once, they are rarely keen to relive the experience!

Warning
Cats are often stung in the mouth, which is dangerous because the resulting swelling can make it difficult for them to breathe. If this happens, consult your vet immediately.

3

WHAT YOUR VET CAN DO

In the case of a bad cut, the wound will have to be cleaned and stitched while your cat is either heavily sedated or anaesthetized, depending on the location and extent of the injury. In the case of stings, bees leave behind the stinging apparatus and, if this can be removed carefully with tweezers or by scraping with the blunt side of a knife, it will bring some relief to the cat.

COMPLEMENTARY TREATMENTS

⬚ HERBAL REMEDIES
After cleaning the wound and trimming any hair which could mat the site, you can apply a solution of calendula to the affected area. Add six drops of tincture to 30 ml (2 tbsp) of water and soak a gauze pad in the mixture. Then tape the gauze carefully in place over the wound.

In the case of minor abrasions, apply a calendula and hypericum ointment to the surface of the wound, which will aid the healing process.

SYSTEMIC ILLNESSES

Systemic illness is defined as a disease of any major organ system or any condition that ultimately affects the whole body. The signs will vary depending on which organ system is involved. The keys to making sure your cat has the greatest possible quality and length of life are early recognition and reduction of any health risk factors, accurate diagnosis and prompt correction to delay progression of the disease. You and your vet will need to regularly monitor your cat's condition to ensure your pet's optimal health.

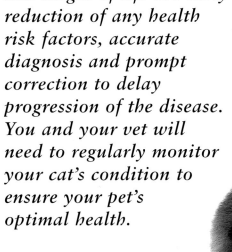

4

THE OLDER CAT

Cats become senior citizens at eight years of age and have special needs just like people do. With advances in veterinary science your cat is likely to live into its twenties and will need increased care and attention to ensure that these years are happy and healthy. Keep stress to a minimum. Older cats are less adaptable to changes in their environment and tend to need more attention to keep them both contented and healthy.

WHAT YOU AND YOUR VET CAN DO

• Feed your senior cat a high-quality diet, specially formulated for its age and lifestyle and try to avoid obesity.

    Seniors need 30 percent fewer calories than when they were younger;
    Cut back on protein and fat;
    Increase fibre to provide bulk so your cat feels full;
    Give dietary supplements (i.e. vitamins, minerals, fresh greens).

• Weigh your cat monthly and keep a record. Subtle weight changes are often the first sign of a problem. Most cats tend toward obesity, though some can become too thin. Progressive weight loss can be a sign of various systemic illnesses such as hyperthyroidism, kidney failure, diabetes, liver disease or cancer.

• Try to ensure that your cat gets 10 minutes exercise twice a day. This is important for weight control and overall health, especially for the heart, lungs and muscles. You can exercise your cat by walking it on a leash or playing games. Check your cat's breathing while it plays—laboured breathing could indicate a respiratory problem.

4

• Consider relocating the litter box for easier access or cutting down its sides so it's easier to get into.

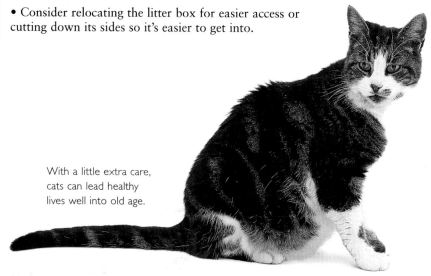

With a little extra care, cats can lead healthy lives well into old age.

• Sick, arthritic or obese cats can't groom themselves properly, so take a little extra time combing and brushing your cat. Regular grooming reduces loose hair and prevents excessive hairball formation. It also stimulates blood circulation in the skin, increases sebaceous gland activity and results in a healthier skin and coat. Trim your cat's nails every two weeks. Many older cats don't use their scratching posts as much.

• Monitor your cat's behaviour and health. Cats are expert at hiding illnesses and the best way of tackling any disorder is early detection and treatment.

• Your vet may suggest a check-up every six months instead of the more usual once a year. During the check-up there will be a thorough physical exam, a check on bodyweight and condition, blood, faecal and urine tests will be done to detect disorders early. A dental exam is essential. Eighty-five percent of cats over eight years have periodontal disease, which can lead to heart disease (see p. 18).

• Arthritis is one of the most common diseases of old age. It can be alleviated with dietary management (i.e. weight loss) and homeopathic remedies.

4

COMPLEMENTARY TREATMENTS

☐ HOMEOPATHIC REMEDIES

Older cats are prone to constipation. If this occurs, *Argentum nitricum* 6c is often prescribed to restore regularity. *Bryonia* is given for arthritis that is worse when the weather is warm. *Rhus tox* is used for arthritis that is worse in cold damp weather. *Causticum* is for severe painful arthritis, joint deformities or muscle weakness.

GLANDULAR DISORDERS

These disorders occur when the endocrine glands, responsible for hormone production, produce either too much or too little of a particular hormone. Thus a shortage of the hormone insulin, produced by the pancreas in response to rising blood sugar levels, results in the condition known as diabetes mellitus. A deficiency of hormone output from the thyroid gland, which affects the rate of metabolism, gives rise to hypothryoidism, whereas an excess leads to hyperthyroidism.

SYMPTOMS

Of diabetes mellitus:
• Signs are not always easy to pick up, particularly in mild cases.
• Increased thirst.
• Larger volume of urine.
• Increased appetite.
• Weight loss.
• Characteristically sweet-smelling breath.

Of hypothyroidism:
• Weight gain.
• Sensitivity to cold.
• Lethargy.
• Thinning coat and scaly skin.

Of hyperthyroidism:
• Increased appetite.
• Matted and scruffy coat.
• Thyroid glands increase in size.
• Increased thirst, often linked with diarrhoea and vomiting.
• Unexplained weight loss.

CAUSES

• Diabetes is caused by damage to the pancreas which may result from obesity, genetic predisposition (e.g. Siamese), or drugs used to treat other conditions. Male cats are more susceptible than females.

• Hypothyroidism is very rare in cats. Hyperthyroidism is often caused by cancer of the thyroid gland. Cats with hyperthyroidism often develop secondary heart and kidney disease, both of which may resolve themselves once the thyroid problem is under control.

4

WHAT YOU AND YOUR VET CAN DO

• If diabetes is suspected, your vet will want to test your cat's blood and urine. The presence of sugar in the blood and urine indicates that cells are having a problem using insulin properly.

• Diabetes is treated by giving your cat a daily injection of insulin and keeping it on carefully monitored diet and fluid intake. Your vet will show you how to do this. It is important to give the injections at the same time every day and the special food at specific times each day as well.

• The diabetic condition may resolve itself in 2–3 months if the cat is properly treated with insulin and the special diet. But you should continue to keep an eye on your pet and watch for any recurrence of symptoms.

• For a thyroid disorder, a blood test will reveal whether the level of thyroid hormone in the blood is too high or too low. The most appropriate treatment for hyperthyroidism will depend on the cat's age and whether it has other medical problems (e.g. heart and kidney disease):

Oral tablets may be prescribed to be given daily. If you have difficulty putting them into your cat's mouth or getting it to swallow, enclose the tablet in a little cheese spread, hold it on your finger and it will lick it off.

Depending on the cat's age and condition, the vet may consider the use of radioactive iodine, a surgical procedure which destroys thyroid tissue. This is thought by many vets to be the best treatment but for the cat owner there is the expense to be taken into account.

If the thyroid gland is cancerous, it can be removed surgically.

4

COMPLEMENTARY TREATMENTS

◪ HERBAL REMEDIES
For diabetes mellitus, sprinkle cool dill or parsley tea over the cat's food. For hyperthyroidism, give horsetail grass tea to replace lost minerals. Immerse 15 ml (1 tbsp) herb or grass in 250 ml (8 fl oz) of hot water, leave to steep for 10 minutes. Allow to cool then pour 15 ml (1 tbsp) of the tea over the food.

◪ DIETARY REMEDIES
Try to increase the vegetable content of your cat's diet with items such as carrots, peas or squash.

◪ BACH FLOWER REMEDIES
A calming treatment using mimulus and impatiens can assist, as hyperthyroid cats are far more active than normal.

None of these remedies are a substitute for hormone replacement. Without insulin, your cat will die.

Parsley tea

LIVER PROBLEMS

The liver, the largest internal organ, is most important to a cat. Its functions include the detoxification of drugs and chemicals, the elimination of toxins and waste products, the production of blood-clotting factors and the secretion of bile, which is necessary for digestion. It also stores fat-soluble vitamins and iron. Because of its wide-ranging tasks any interference with the way the liver works can be very serious. In a cat, it is easily damaged by various conditions. Inflammation of the liver is called hepatitis, which can come from a number of causes. Fatty liver disease or hepatic lipidosis is an excessive accumulation of fat in the liver cells; it is common in cats.

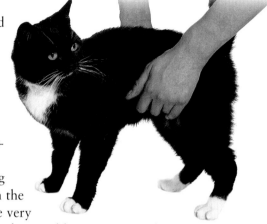

4

SYMPTOMS

- Lack of appetite.
- Weight loss.
- Depression.
- Jaundice—a yellowish discoloration of the whites of the eyes.
- Dark, discoloured urine (caused by accumulation of bile pigment).
- Increased thirst.
- Abdominal swelling (from fluid build-up).
- Vomiting.

CAUSES

• The cause of hepatic lipidosis is as yet unknown, but cats that don't eat for several days are at the most risk.

• Hepatitis can be caused by infections, either bacterial or viral (see Feline Peritonitis, p. 31), toxins, poisons or secondary to heart disease.

WHAT YOU AND YOUR VET CAN DO

• Your vet may have to perform a biopsy (removing a small part of the liver tissue for laboratory examination) to determine the cause.

• Diet is the most important factor in treatment. A carefully controlled diet lessens the work of the liver, allowing it to recover. Provide high-value protein, such as egg, and offer the cat food in small amounts throughout the day.

• For hepatic lipidosis due to anorexia, force-feeding may be necessary.

YOUR CAT'S DIGESTIVE ORGANS

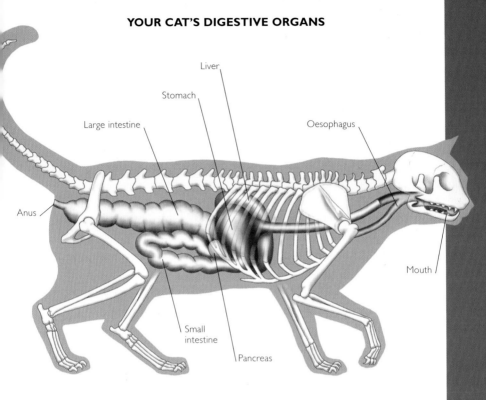

Liver

Stomach

Large intestine

Oesophagus

Anus

Mouth

Small
intestine

Pancreas

COMPLEMENTARY TREATMENTS

4

✕ DIETARY REMEDIES

Vitamin supplements are beneficial for cats with both hepatitis and lipidosis. To stimulate the cat's appetite try a mixture of honey and yogurt.
Raw liver given once a week supplies vitamins and iron.

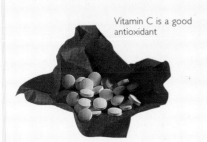

Vitamin C is a good antioxidant

✕ HERBAL REMEDIES

Chopped parsley sprinkled over the cat's food may be helpful.

▢ HOMEOPATHIC REMEDIES

The tissue salt *Natrum sulphuricum* 6x (sodium sulphate) is frequently given to cats suffering from liver problems. This ought to result in an improvement in 24 hours.

Another acute treatment can be provided by *Belladonna* 6x (deadly nightshade), which is especially indicated in cases of fever. Where the cat is thirsty and yet vomits, *Bryonia* 6x (wild hops) may be prescribed.

KIDNEY PROBLEMS

The kidneys filter and remove toxic waste products from the cat's blood via the urine. They also regulate calcium and vitamin D levels, maintain the cat's level of hydration and secrete the hormone responsible for red blood cell production. Acute kidney disease occurs suddenly and is rare in cats but, with prompt recognition and treatment, it is generally reversible. Chronic kidney disease occurs as the kidneys deteriorate slowly over a cat's lifetime. This is a most common situation and is called chronic renal disease (CRD). CRD is not reversible and the signs generally don't occur until 80 percent of kidney function is lost.

CAUSES

- Most usual: progressive age-related deterioration of the kidneys.

- Bacterial and viral infections.

- Nutritional factors, e.g. obesity.

- Immune system defect as in leukaemia, feline AIDS or cancer.

- Toxins, such as antifreeze.

- Inherited breed defects, e.g. the Abyssinian.

4

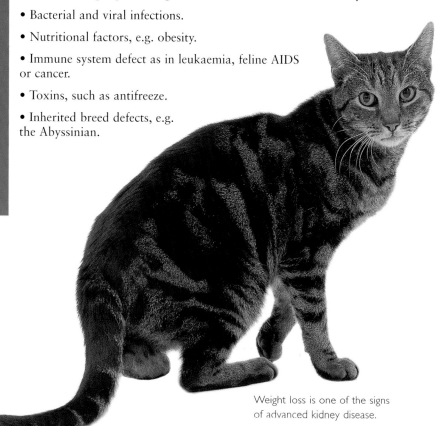

Weight loss is one of the signs of advanced kidney disease.

WHAT YOU AND YOUR VET CAN DO

• Blood and urine tests will enable your vet to assess the severity of the condition and provide advice on how to stabilize it. The vet may do an X ray, ultrasound scan or biopsy to aid diagnosis.

• Fluid replacement is central to supportive care for cats with malfunctioning kidneys. Always make sure that the cat's waterbowl is full of clean water.

• You can assess the state of dehydration by pinching the cat's skin on the top of the neck for 5 seconds and then seeing how long it takes to flatten. The skin should pop back in 1–3 seconds. If it does not, the cat needs to be rehydrated. Rehydration can be done by your vet by subcutaneous injection or intravenously.

• Good nutrition is also vital. The goal is to decrease the workload on the kidneys by decreasing the amount of waste the kidneys must eliminate. Excess dietary protein, phosphorus and salt create a lot of waste so it's best to give your cat a diet that contains small amounts of high quality protein, e.g. eggs, and foods low in salt and low in phosphorus. Special diets can be bought from pet stores and the contents will be listed on them.

• Most cats with kidney failure are also anaemic (see p. 80) and will need B vitamins and iron. Brewer's yeast and raw liver are good sources.

• Anti-hypertensive drugs (derived from human medicine) are now being given to cats to prevent further deterioration of the kidneys.

SYMPTOMS

• Increased urination.
• Increased thirst
• Decreased appetite.
• Dehydration.
• Depression.
• Weakness.
• Vomiting.

4

COMPLEMENTARY TREATMENTS

⊠ HERBAL REMEDIES
Two drops of alfalfa tincture three times daily, may be recommended. This can reduced to once daily as the condition stabilizes.

☐ HOMEOPATHIC REMEDIES
Natrum muriaticum 200c (sodium chloride) can be helpful. Higher potencies may be needed in due course, to 10m or beyond. Eel serum should promote urinary flow, helping to ensure the kidneys can continue to function adequately.

Relief can also be provided by *Apis mellifica* 10m. Four doses administered at hourly intervals are normally recommended. *Apis mellifica* should be avoided if your cat is pregnant.

Apis mellifica is made from the honey bee.

URINARY TRACT PROBLEMS

Urine from the kidneys passes down tubes called ureters to the bladder, where it is stored, before being voided via the urethra. Feline lower urinary tract diseases, called FLUTD, are very common in cats, affecting the bladder (cystitis) and the urethra (urethritis).

CAUSES

• Bacterial or viral infection.

• Plugs of mineral material in the urethra.

• Small stones known as calculi may form within the urinary tract, or stones may stem from the kidneys themselves.

An electron micrograph of a kidney stone.

Warning

Observe your cat urinating, because this is when problems are most likely to be apparent.
The cat will strain to urinate and the pain may produce a hunched appearance and cries of discomfort.
It will urinate frequently with small amounts of urine or none at all.
Spayed female cats often have blood in the urine.
Neutered male cats may get a blockage: this is very serious and a medical emergency.

• It is most important that your cat should have constant access to clean fresh water. Dehydration is serious and will cause urinary tract disorders.

• Stress.

• In more than half of cases, no underlying cause is found.

WHAT YOU AND YOUR VET CAN DO

• The vet will diagnose the problem with blood and urine tests. Your observations as owner will be vital in this situation.

• Treatment is focused on management of the diet and environment to minimize the problem, which will tend to recur.

• Cats that seem predisposed to feline lower urinary tract disease are overweight, neutered male and spayed female cats with an alkaline (pH over 7) urine. A diet should be devised that promotes acidic urine and has low levels of magnesium and ash and there are proprietary diets that supply this.

• Try feeding several small meals during the day and be sure your cat drinks plenty of water.

• Follow the advice under obesity (p. 32) to try to ameliorate these conditions.

4

THE URINARY SYSTEM

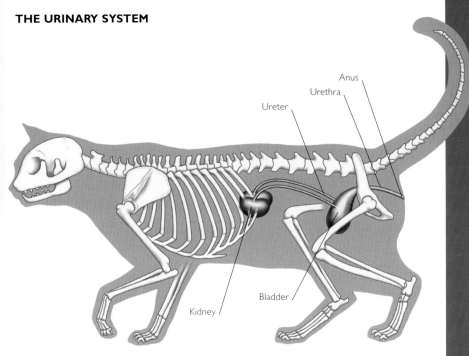

Anus

Urethra

Ureter

Bladder

Kidney

4

COMPLEMENTARY TREATMENTS

⊠**HERBAL REMEDIES**
For cystitis and urethritis:
Couchgrass tea, 15 ml (1 tbsp) twice
daily (how to
make, p. 69).
Birch leaf tea,
5 ml (1 tsp)
twice daily.

Mix one-third tsp twice a day of nettles,
golden seal, buchu (*Agathosma* spp.) and
flax seed.

□**HOMEOPATHIC REMEDIES**
Pulsatilla 30c, 1 pellet every four hours
up to three times, for cystitis.
   Sarsparilla 30c, 3 pellets at 15 minute
intervals, for male cats having problems
urinating.
   Canthans 30c, 3 pellets at 15 minute
intervals, for male cats having problems
urinating.

⊠**DIETARY REMEDIES**
Fresh cranberry juice, left, can bring
relief from cystitis if your cat will
drink it.

REPRODUCTIVE PROBLEMS

You should consider carefully, when you get your kitten or adult cat, whether you want to breed from it. If you don't, it is probably better to have the cat neutered. This eliminates unwanted pregnancies, the possibility of cancer of the reproductive tract and, in male cats, reduces aggression and urine spraying. Cats generally have few problems during pregnancy. A typical litter is four or five kittens, born after roughly 64 days. Queens are sometimes unable to produce enough milk, posssibly because of infection of the mammary glands.

WHAT YOU AND YOUR VET CAN DO

• Male cats should ideally be neutered at about six months. The testes are removed under anaesthetic and the cat will be back to normal very quickly.

• Spaying the female cat is done at around four or five months. Most female cats are mature enough to reproduce by six months of age. The uterus, ovaries and fallopian tubes are removed under anaesthetic. A patch of hair is generally shaved from the cat's abdomen and it will have several stitches but will show very little discomfort. Spaying completely eliminates the cat's heat cycles, nervousness and desire to mate.

• Always keep a close watch on a cat that has just given birth. The uterus can become the site of infection in the period immediately after the birth, and if bacteria start to multiply here the queen will soon fall ill.

• If the mother cat develops an infection, rapid treatment is needed, not only to safeguard her health, but also that of the kittens, which may have to be hand-reared while their mother is incapacitated (see p. 98). In addition to the use of antibiotics, the vet may also administer the hormone oxytocin to encourage contractions of the uterus. These drugs will help to dislodge any placentas left here, and empty its contents. In more severe cases, fluid therapy may also be required.

• A vet will usually prescribe antibiotics in the case of mastitis.

4

SYMPTOMS

Mastitis:
• One or more mammary glands feels hot and painful.
• Reluctance to suckle.

Sexual behavioural problems:
• Excessive male territorial marking and aggression.
• In breed females, persistent calling when on heat

Warning

It is not just during or immediately after pregnancy that reproductive problems can develop. Pyometra is a particularly insidious and life-threatening infection of the uterus, which can affect older female cats that have never been pregnant.

If the kittens are noisy and restless while feeding, it could mean that the mother is not producing enough milk.

4

COMPLEMENTARY TREATMENTS

⊠ HERBAL REMEDIES

Raspberry leaf tablets are a traditional means of helping to ensure a trouble-free labour. They are normally given from the third week of pregnancy until the seventh week.

▭ HOMEOPATHIC REMEDIES

Viburnum opulus 30c (water elder), given twice a week during the first month of pregnancy, is recommended to try to ensure the continuation of a pregnancy.

Arnica montana 30c (leopard's bane) can help a queen recuperate rapidly after giving birth.

Urtica urens 30c (stinging nettle) should be given three times daily for five days if the queen has a shortage of milk for her kittens.

In cases of acute mastitis, *Belladonna* 6c (deadly nightshade) is recommended. A normal dosage is five successive doses every two hours. Chronic mastitis often responds better to *Silicea* 200c, prepared from silicon dioxide. This is usually given twice weekly for six weeks.

HEART PROBLEMS

The heart is the most important organ in the body. Its function is to collect oxygen-poor blood from the body and pump it to the lungs to pick up oxygen. The heart then pumps the oxygen-rich blood back out into the body. Cardiomyopathy is the most common heart disease in cats, affecting the heart muscle so that it cannot pump blood effectively. Circulation is impaired and certain tissues are then deprived of oxygen and vital nutrients. Cardiomyopathy occurs in different forms and is most common in young pure-bred cats. It occurs suddenly with almost no warning and needs immediate veterinary attention.

SYMPTOMS

In most cases, there are very few signs until the disease is advanced. Owners may notice in the cat:
• Shortness of breath or difficulty breathing.
• Weakness and decrease in activity.
• Blueish tongue and gums.
• Coughing or gagging.
• Loss of appetite.
• Fainting or sudden collapse.
• Difficulty walking or paralysis of the hind legs due to blood clot formation.

CAUSES

• Failing heart muscle (cardiomyopathy).

• Heartworm disease, caused by worms living in the heart. This is transmitted by mosquito bites and causes sudden death. No treatment is available.

• Taurine deficiency. Taurine is an essential amino acid that is occasionally absent in the diet, but deficiency is rare as most proprietary diets are taurine-enriched. Raw liver is a good natural source.

• Other causes of malfunction can be cancer or hyperthyroidism (see p. 68).

• Hereditary factors, which is why it is more common in pure-bred cats.

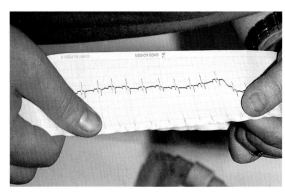

The readings of a cat electrocardiogram (ECG).

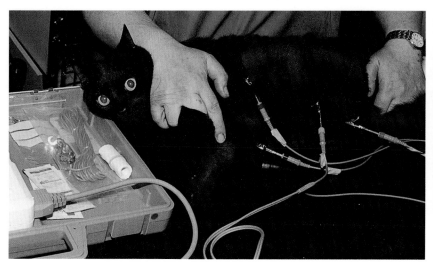

A cat having an ECG will probably have to be calmed and held, by someone it trusts.

WHAT YOU AND YOUR VET CAN DO

• Your vet will diagnose the problem with a electrocardiogram (ECG) or X ray examination of the chest.

• Most cats with heart conditions respond poorly to treatment and tend to develop blood clots.

• The decreased blood flow to the kidneys affects their function and so there is an accumulation of fluid, possibly in the lungs. Diuretics can be prescribed to remove fluid—the cat will urinate more frequently as a result.

• A low sodium diet is often recommended. If your water is soft, give the cat ditilled water as soft water is often high in sodium. Low sodium diets decrease blood pressure and therefore the risk of heart attacks.

• Antioxidant vitamins can slow heart disease—vitamins C, E and A.

4

COMPLEMENTARY TREATMENTS	
⊠ HERBAL REMEDIES	**▢ HOMEOPATHIC REMEDIES**
Parsley tea can be given in conjunction with a diuretic to increase fluid loss from the body. Add a few sprigs of parsley to boiling water. Allow to stand for 10 minutes. Strain and allow to cool. Pour 15 ml (1 tbsp) of the tea over the cat's food.	*Crataegus oxycantha* 3x, one pellet a day for 30 days, for weak heart. *Digitalis purpurea* 6x may improve heart function. *Spongia tosta* 6x, one a day for 30 days. None of these treatments is a substitute for veterinary care.

ANAEMIA

Anaemia results from a low number of red cells in the circulation. It can be life-threatening because the red blood cells, produced in the bone marrow, are responsible for carrying oxygen around the body. Anaemia can arise from a wide range of causes, from the comparatively harmless, such as flea infestation, to an underlying serious malfunction of the organs.

SYMPTOMS

- Lack of energy.
- Pale gums and eye membranes.

CAUSES

- Infestations of blood-sucking parasites, such as fleas, lice or hookworms. It is important to detect this early in kittens as the blood loss can be fatal.

- Viruses such as feline leukaemia virus (FLV) or feline AIDS. Vaccination (see p. 11) will afford some protection against leukaemia which is potentially fatal. The virus not only attacks bone marrow, but also destroys red blood cells.

- Kidney disease (see p. 72).

- Trauma causing blood loss.

4

WHAT YOU AND YOUR VET CAN DO

- The vet will take a blood sample to determine the severity of the problem, and give an appropriate treatment.

- If the anaemia is severe, then a blood transfusion may be necessary. Most cats have type A blood.

- Your vet will recommend a diet high in vitamins, iron and protein. Liver is a good source of protein, and vitamin B, green vegetables and kelp provide iron, and 500 mg of vitamin C should be given daily.

COMPLEMENTARY TREATMENTS

☑ HOMEOPATHIC REMEDIES
Chena officinalis 6c, one pellet daily for 30 days, is good for weakness after blood loss.

Calcium phosphate can be given for anaemia and malnutrition.

BEHAVIOURAL PROBLEMS

As with most animals, the character of cats varies, both between individuals and between different breeds. You should take this into consideration when choosing a pet. Generally, cats are self-sufficient, clean and quiet, but behavioural problems can arise. This is less likely if you choose a kitten as it can be encouraged from the start to behave properly in the home and toward other pets. If your cat is older, there are ways of dealing with behavioural problems, especially if you can find out the underlying cause. For example, if it was mistreated in the past it may have developed a fear of people. If you are taking a cat from a rescue group, get as much of its history as possible.

SOCIALIZATION

Socialization is learning to adjust your instincts to the world you live in. In the case of a cat the key is helping it to become familiar with people, other animals and things in their surroundings. It requires training and consistency with lots of love and plenty of patience.

WHAT YOU CAN DO

• To socialize your kitten, take it everywhere you go, introduce it to as many new people, places, sights, sounds and smells as possible. Kittens are like children and need plenty of stimulus to grow into happy lively creatures.

• Play plenty of games with it. Most cats like games that stimulate their natural instincts, enjoying chasing and pouncing.

• Start from day one. It's important to realize that, when you give the kitten a toy to play with, a post to scratch or a litter box to use, you're also teaching it what is all right to play with and scratch, as well as indicating the place where its business must be done.

• The best way to start socialization is with positive reinforcement. Observe your cat's natural behaviour. Try to find out what it likes to do best. Reward it for 'good' behaviour with special food, a treat perhaps, a game with its favourite toy, or physical affection, belly rubs or ear scratching.

• Negative reinforcement can be used to discourage it from doing what is dangerous—kittens sometimes like to chew on electric wiring—or destructive about the home. Negative reinforcements include sprinkling the cat with a little water or making a loud sudden noise by, for example, rattling a can filled with pennies. It is important to take your kitten's character into account when using negative reinforcement as you may cause it to be frightened rather than getting the message. Most kittens are bold enough when they are confident that they are loved!

The African wild cat is considered to be the ancestor of the domestic cat.

5

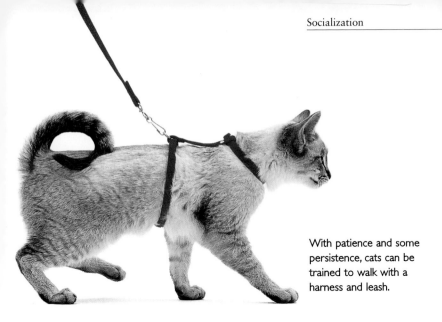

With patience and some
persistence, cats can be
trained to walk with a
harness and leash.

• If you get your cat as an adult, you will probably need more patience to
deal with any problems that arise. They may, for instance, result from
past traumas that you know nothing about. You should not forget that
moving to a new home, especially if there are other pets already there,
is a very stressful experience for a cat.

• If you opt for a pure-bred cat, you should realize that there are significant
differences between them in terms of temperament, which in turn can
affect the type of behavioural problems to which they are susceptible.
Siamese cats are highly active and demonstrative by nature, while larger
breeds such as Persian Longhairs tend to be much more phlegmatic and are
calmer in their ways.

• Unravelling the cause of a behavioural problem is not always
straightforward, but the best place to start is to seek your vet's advice, in
case there is an underlying medical problem.

COMPLEMENTARY TREATMENTS

5

◫ HOMEOPATHIC REMEDIES
Bach flower Rescue Remedy can help
to alleviate stress. Two drops directly
into the mouth is usual, up to 3 times
a day. Anti-anxiety medications can
also be given.

BEHAVIOURAL TRAINING

Despite your best efforts, many behavioural problems cannot be prevented and require treatment. Behavioural modification methods vary from reinforcements that you can do at home, usually needing much repetition and patience, to veterinary treatment ranging from tranquillizers to hormones.

WHAT YOU AND YOUR VET CAN DO

• At home, you can use positive reinforcement (see p. 82) to reward good behaviour or negative reinforcement to discourage antisocial behaviour.

• If your cat persists in chewing or clawing furniture, attacking other pets or acting aggressively toward you or other people, you must try to discourage it gently with something that does not frighten it but just makes it uncomfortable. Some cats respond best to a squirt of water; others to a sudden loud noise. In the second instance, ensure that the cat does not associate the loud noise directly with you. Don't look at the cat while you are doing it and it will blame the noise, not you.

• If your cat persists in chewing electrical wiring or houseplants, you can spray the area with strong scent or cologne and dab hot pepper sauce on whatever it is chewing. Cats hate strong perfume smells so this is a good way of deterring persistent problems.

• Never physically punish your pet. It will blame you and won't forgive you.

5

This posture, with ears flattened to the head, is typical of a frightened or stressed cat.

• Your vet may use psychotropic medication as a last resort to deal with psychological problems. Anti-anxiety medications can be used to reduce fear and anxiety during periods of adjustment—such as a new pet or new baby in the home, moving house, or sharing with holiday guests. Mild tranquillizers can be prescribed by your vet to reduce aggression. For such states as Feline Endocrine Alopecia, which comes from compulsive overgrooming for whatever reason, a hormone would be the most likely treatment.

• Remember that many behavioural problems can spring from hormonal activity in your cat, most of which is related to reproduction. If you are sure that you do not want to breed from your cat, you should talk to the vet about having it neutered. In a female particularly it can reduce obsessive behaviour which can be irritating to you as the owner.

COMPLEMENTARY TREATMENTS

▢ HOMEOPATHIC REMEDIES
Although it is important to try to prevent the causes of stress as far as possible, this is not always feasible. If your cat is injured in a fight, then *Arnica montana* 6c (leopard's bane) can bring relief.

▨ BACH FLOWER REMEDIES
Use the Bach flower Rescue Remedy, made of cherry plum, clematis, impatiens, rock rose and star of Bethlehem to calm the cat in cases of acute stress or shock.

5

LITTER TRAY PROBLEMS

Failing to use the litter box is the number one behavioural problem with cats. You should first of all check the cat out with the vet so that the presence of a lower urinary tract disease can be ruled out. There may also be abnormally active urine spraying involved (see p. 88). Litter box aversion occurs when the cat prefers to use other surfaces, often the bathroom or kitchen work surfaces. It can be a difficult problem to solve. The way forward is to be patient and try to work out the reason why the cat does not want to use its box.

CAUSES

• When kittens become sexually mature (at about five or six months) they may start to spray urine. This is natural territorial behaviour and will stop with neutering or spaying.

• The introduction of another cat to the household can result in your established pet relieving itself in a variety of locations around the home. This is territorial marking activity because your pet feels threatened.

Nervous cats in particular are likely to be dissuaded by a lack of privacy, so a hooded litter tray is recommended.

• In some cases, the cause of litter tray problems may not be immediately obvious. If you have a cat flap, for example, it could well be that one or several other cats from the neighbourhood are entering your home, unknown to you, spraying and causing distress to your pet.

• Some older cats, especially those suffering from arthritis, which makes movement painful, may find it difficult and uncomfortable to step over the sides of the litter tray, so they soil the area nearby instead.

WHAT YOU CAN DO

• It is essential to keep the tray clean. Scoop it out daily, especially after the cat has used it—it won't come back to it otherwise. Change the litter completely every 3–5 days.

• Use plain litters which are not scented and do not clump when wet. Choose one that is suitable for your sewage system.

• If your cat is an outdoor cat coming to live inside, try filling the tray with potting compost.

> **Warning**
>
> While it is important to disinfect the tray regularly, be sure to wash off any chemicals thoroughly. An off-putting odour that remains is more than likely to deter the cat.

• Make sure the tray is in a quiet part of your home, where there is little or no traffic. Get a cover for the box, or a screen. Don't put the tray near where the cat sleeps or eats.

• If your cat is too stiff to climb into the litter tray without difficulty, it may be necessary to cut away part of a side, leaving a slight rim, to give it easier access. Standing the tray on sheets of newspaper will help to catch any litter scraped out through the opening.

• In a multi-cat household, the minimum should be one box for two cats.

• Don't use an ammonia-based disinfectant to clean up mistakes. Cat urine contains ammonia and the cat will be even more attracted to the spot.

Cats are sensitive animals, and they need to feel safe and secure while they relieve themselves. Make sure their litter tray is in a relatively quiet spot.

5

URINE SPRAYING

Urine spraying occurs with sexual maturity, at about six months of age, especially in intact males. Normally, cats urinate squatting but spraying is done on vertical surfaces while standing. Outdoors, male cats spray on prominent landmarks such as fence posts, returning to the same spots regularly to reinforce their marks as rain dilutes them. Similar behaviour in the home is almost inevitable in the case of mature toms and is very unpleasant, as the odour is difficult to eliminate, even with the use of proprietary products. Female cats may also spray, usually when they are ready to breed. Their urine then contains chemicals called pheromones, to attract male cats in the neighbourhood.

CAUSES

• A cat's instinctive need to mark its territory.

• Spraying is a normal behaviour but can be due to stress or anxiety.

WHAT YOU AND YOUR VET CAN DO

• The only successful long-term solution for male cats is likely to be neutering, which is a relatively simple operation, although it does require a general anaesthetic.

• The best time for neutering depends to an extent on the type of cat you have, especially since many owners like the jowls, characteristic of heavier breeds such as the British and American Shorthairs. Their skin folds around the face are a secondary sexual characteristic, and develop in male cats as a result of puberty. Neutering too early means that the jowls do not have a chance to develop.

5

Warning

If your cat suddenly starts spraying urine around the home, it is important to seek veterinary advice. It could be indicative of a medical problem, such as cystitis or even diabetes mellitus, which needs professional attention.

• For more precocious breeds, such as the Siamese, neutering can be done earlier as they do not have jowls (see p. 76).

• For female cats, spaying generally resolves the problem, as well as preventing unwanted kittens being born.

• You should realize that surgery may not immediately overcome the problem of spraying. In older cats, it takes six weeks for the hormone levels to decrease in the blood and time is needed for the learned behaviour pattern to be forgotten.

• Responsibility for triggering spraying may lie with you if you have previously come in contact with another cat that has twined itself around your legs and left a scent that is discernible to your pet. Its territorial instinct will take over and it may spray a chair leg, for example, in your vicinity.

• When you move house, check whether the previous occupants owned a cat, because this can cause repeated spraying as your cat tries to mask the scent left by its predecessor. Prevention is the simplest answer in this case. You should arrange for any carpets to be cleaned thoroughly and any tiled or wooden flooring or linoleum to be washed. Always remember that your cat's sense of smell is much greater than your own.

Neutering is the only successful long-term solution to urine spraying.

5

DESTRUCTIVE BEHAVIOUR

Scratching is a natural grooming behaviour that keeps your cat's claws in good shape and is another way for cats mark their territory. Unfortunately, it can also ruin your furniture and destroy your home. A cat will also chew on houseplants, especially when a kitten, which is both destructive and potentially dangerous to your pet.

WHAT YOU CAN DO

• To prevent the development of bad scratching habits, get a scratching post when you get a cat. Keep lots of the cat's toys near it and put it in a place the cat likes, e.g. a favourite window or the room the family uses. You can also rub catnip into it or put a catnip ball at the top. If you make your own scratching post, cats like loosely woven material such as hemp, or you can cover a post with carpeting.

• Observe your cat and when it scratches. It will usually be when they wake up or when you, their owner, come home. Place the scratching post near the cat's bed or beside the front door.

Your kitten will imitate its mother's behaviour. You should check the mother's habits before you buy one of her kittens.

5

• Your kitten's mother is its best teacher so, before getting a kitten, ask the owner if its mother uses a scratching post regularly.

• Trim your cat's nails regularly, every 3–4 weeks (see p. 60).

LAST RESORTS

• You can get your vet to apply vinyl nail caps.

• It is possible for the vet to perform an operation to remove the claws, but this deprives the cat of a part of its natural behaviour and also leaves it defenceless. Better alternatives would be to keep the cat outside if possible or take it to an animal shelter.

PLANT EATING

• Lots of cats eat grass and houseplants. Grass is fine but lots of houseplants are toxic (see p. 100).

WHAT YOU CAN DO

• Provide safe, edible green plants for your cat to eat.

• Move non-edible plants out of reach.

• Use negative reinforcement methods to help the cat to discriminate between the plants that it can eat, from yours (see p. 82). If plants cannot be moved out of reach, dab the leaves with hot pepper sauce or spray strong cologne round them. That should deter it!

5

AGGRESSION

The most common cause of feline aggression is the introduction of a new cat into the home. If this is planned carefully, you can avoid a lot of trouble for yourself. It is nearly always the case that cats that act aggressively toward people are either overly playful or irritated for some reason.

INTRODUCING A NEW CAT INTO THE HOME

• The process should be very gradual, taking from two to three weeks.

• First, keep the cats in separate rooms with a closed door between them until they get used to each other's smell.

• Next, let them meet in the same room, each on a harness. The cats should be held on the laps of two people 2–3 metres (8–10 feet) apart. Do this twice daily for 10-15 minute sessions, moving the chairs gradually closer.

• When all seems well, let the cats loose.

Remember:
• Provide an escape route, e.g. an open door, so that neither cat feels trapped.
• Spend a lot of time with the cat that was there first.

5

When holding a cat, always support its hindquarters so that it feels safe. This is particularly important for cats that are not used to being held.

COUNTERING AGGRESSION

• If your cat suddenly develops aggressive behaviour, consult your vet. It may be due to a medical problem causing it pain when handled.

• A rescued cat may have been maltreated in the past, making it wary of being handled. Patience and frequent, gentle handling are called for in a situation like this.

• Over-playful cats should be provided with plenty of moving, dangling toys.

• Aggression toward you may be redirected aggression toward another cat. Give it time on its own and avoid eye contact.

• Always make sure you use a carrier made specifically for cats. It should be both secure and well ventilated and types vary. You might prefer a top-loading one which allows you to remove a cat more easily. After a journey your cat will soon relax when it is back on familiar territory. There is no need to persuade it to leave its carrier. Simply open the top and let your pet come out in its own time.

Warning

When transporting your cat in a car, line the base of the carrier with a thick layer of newspaper, which is highly absorbent. Then, if your cat has an accident, its urine will not leave a lingering unpleasant odour in the vehicle.

COMPLEMENTARY TREATMENTS

☐ HOMEOPATHIC REMEDIES
Skullcap and valerian tablets given before a journey should help to calm a nervous individual.

Bach Rescue Remedy decreases anxiety.

5

OBSESSIVE BEHAVIOUR

Cats are very much creatures of habit. They like stable and tranquil surroundings and a non hectic lifestyle. They also like to stick to a routine. If obsessive behaviour appears you can assume that the causes will either be physical or psychological—that is, the cat is stressed or anxious. The problems are most common in multi-cat households and pure-breds are more susceptible to them than others.

TYPES OF OBSESSIVE BEHAVIOUR

• Wool-chewing: adult Siamese and Burmese cats will sometimes start chewing or sucking woollen sweaters or other materials. This is sometimes because they were weaned too early, or it can be that their diet lacks the vegetable fibre that they need, or simply that they are feeling stressed. They will often chew up entire garments or blankets, which can be a costly problem.

• Overgrooming: otherwise called Feline Endocrine Alopecia. This again is most common in adult Siamese. Signs to look for are bald, hairless areas particularly in the groin and hind end. The cat will be seen licking itself obsessively and pulling at its own fur.

WHAT YOU CAN DO

• To combat wool-chewing, you can add fibre to your cat's diet with fresh vegetables and chopped greens, or get some edible plants especially for your cat. Some pet stores sell roughage-rich plants. Or you can try strips of tough meat which gives it something to chew on.

• You can try behavioural modification methods (see p. 84), as well as playing more with your cat and giving it extra care and treats for good behaviour.

5

Give your cat lots of extra care and attention in potentially stressful times.

Warning

While such behaviour may seem compulsive, grass eating may be indicative of an underlying health problem (see p. 28). Should your cat regularly eat grass, this normally indicates there is an obstruction, such as a hairball or an accumulation of roundworms.

• Increase the time you spend grooming your pet. Brush it a lot. You might also give it laxatives to decrease hairball formation which result from overgrooming.

• Try to work out what it is about your cat's environment that might be causing stress or anxiety. The cat may be feeling threatened by a strange cat in your area or a new cat, or even a child, in the home.

• You should take the cat to the vet to rule out a medical problem such as flea allergy or a hormonal problem.

• As a last resort, you could talk to your vet about whether medication would be appropriate to relieve stress (see p. 84).

5

HUNTING

Cats have an instinctive desire to hunt, although this drive is stronger in some types than others. For example, pure-bred cats, which have been bred in catteries for many generations, are less likely to hunt. Domestication and regular meals mean that for most cats today, the need to hunt has been removed. By returning to you with offerings, the cat is seeking to reinforce its bond with you and your family.

Warning

If you are able to rescue a bird or another creature alive from your cat, remember it will be in a state of shock, and handling should be kept to an absolute minimum. Put the creature in a dark place and seek veterinary advice. The outlook is often poor, even if the injury is not severe. This is because the bacteria injected into the body by the cat's bite are often likely to cause fatal septicaemia.

WHAT YOU CAN DO

Apart from keeping your cat permanently indoors, there is very little you can do to stop it hunting. If your cat is not neutered, this operation can reduce the hunting instinct. There are several measures you can take that may make your cat less successful in its endeavours.

• Try fitting your cat with an elasticated collar which has a bell to warn off potential prey. The elasticity in the collar is vital so that the cat does not become caught up, on a branch, for instance, and strangled.

• If you want to feed birds in your garden, hang food on thin twigs that the cat can't climb. Never throw scraps on the lawn. That's asking for trouble.

• It may be dangerous for your cat to play with certain things it has caught. Kittens will hunt wasps or bees and may get stung. Toads can eject toxins from their skin and, if there are poisonous snakes in your area, your cat may get bitten. In these cases, immediate veterinary treatment may be necessary.

5

FIRST AID

To help ensure the health of your cat and your family, preventive measures and common sense are needed. It's a good idea to have a first aid kit, to learn a few first aid techniques, to be familiar with poisons and keep them out of reach. Keep a list of emergency phone numbers on hand including your vet's phone number and a 24-hour care facility number. Always consult your vet before giving medicines to your cat and never give it medicines meant for people. If your cat develops a chronic condition, such as diabetes or leukaemia, keep a written record of all medications and important notes about the condition.

BIRTH AND RAISING KITTEN:

Generally, it is better to get a kitten from a breeder or animal recue centre as there are always plenty of cats and kittens needing homes. However, you may find yourself looking after a cat that is in kitten, perhaps a stray. In most cases, queens give birth to their litter without any problems, but difficulties can crop up occasionally, in which case rapid intervention will be necessary to safeguard the welfare of both the queen and her offspring. Pregnancy normally lasts on average about 64 days. At the end of this time, provide a quiet location where she can give birth and do not let her wander off outside, where it will be much harder to check on her health and that of her kittens. Occasionally, a mother will reject her kittens or a kitten for medical or psychological reasons or she may not survive giving birth and you will have to raise the kittens yourself.

RAISING ORPHAN KITTENS

• For the first two weeks of life, kittens can't regulate their own body temperature and need to be kept warm at 24–27°C (80–85°F).

• They need to be fed every few hours for the first week. Commercial formulas are available or you can make one by combining 220 ml (8 fl oz) of fresh milk, one egg, 30 ml (2 tbsp) of honey and an appropriate vitamin/mineral supplement. Warm the formula to your body temperature 37°C (98.6°F)—test a few drops on your wrist.

• You can use an eyedropper or a nursing bottle. Special kitten nursing bottles are available, designed to keep air bubbles out of the kitten's stomach.

• Most kittens weigh from 50–100 g (2–4 oz) at birth. They require about 8ml (just under 2 tsp) of formula per 25 g (1 oz) of bodyweight per 24 hours. divide this amount into feeds given every 3–4 hours.

• Later, feeding every 6–8 hours will be enough. At 3–4 weeks, when the kittens have teeth, offer small amounts of canned food mixed with milk. They should be fully weaned at 8 weeks.

Warning

Frequent meals and warmth are absolutely vital in the first weeks of the kitten's life.

6

HYPOTHERMIA

Thanks to their dense coats, cats are able to survive in very cold environments, although there are significant differences in this respect between breeds such as the Maine Coon, which are well protected against the cold with their dense underfur, and breeds from more tropical parts of the world that have have thinner coats. Even so, cats do suffer from hypothermia on occasion, and it is not just outside on a cold day that this problem can arise. They can also suffer from frostbite on their extremities—the ears, paws and tail.

CAUSES

• Hypothermia can be a sign of severe shock. If you find a cat that has collapsed, it could be that hypothermia has set in—this can be gauged by taking the cat's temperature. A normal reading is approximately 39°C (102°F). Of course, it is important to ascertain what caused the shock initially, and in this case it is best to consult your vet immediately.

• If a cat has become badly chilled as a result of being trapped in freezing water, it will have lost the benefit of insulation from its underfur, as the water will have driven the air out from here.

WHAT YOU AND YOUR VET CAN DO

• A brisk rub with a towel should help to bring back signs of life. Move the cat into warm surroundings as soon as possible, but the temperature should not be too hot because this will draw blood from the body's organs to the skin, worsening the shock. Instead, allow the cat to warm up gradually.

• Special low wattage heat pads—sold in pet shops—which fit beneath the cat's bed will provide a localized source of heat. Cover the cat with towels or blankets to build up its body heat again. Do not use a hot water bottle as a heat source; it could burn the cat if it is not able to move easily.

• For frostbitten paws, dip them in warm—not hot—water. The paws may be painful as they 'come round' so handle your cat carefully.

6

DANGERS IN THE HOME

There are various aspects of your home that can present a hazard to your cat. Cats are naturally curious and adventurous and will taste or chew anything within reach. You must bear this in mind when choosing and locating your houseplants, your decorations and, if practicably possible, your electric cables. In addition, many household drugs are toxic to cats. Never give your cat any drugs not formulated for pets and do not leave them lying around.

HOUSEPLANT HAZARDS

• Cats rarely get seriously ill from chewing plants but can make themselves sick. Indoor plants which can cause upset include azaleas, foxgloves, philodendrons, cyclamens, Jerusalem cherries, Dieffenbachias, Spiderplants, Dragon trees, Airplane plants (Crassula) and Caladiums. Cats often vomit after chewing plants. This is not necessarily important. Only severe or persistent vomiting is a danger sign (see p. 28).

• Keep houseplants out of reach as far as possible and provide alternatives of fresh edible greens such as parsley for your cat to chew on.

HOLIDAY HAZARDS

• Other hazards can be encountered at holiday periods. Christmas ornament fragments can perforate the stomach. Cats are very prone to chewing string, tinsel and ribbon. If this is ingested, it can cause painful intestinal problems. In addition, pine needles from Christmas trees can also perforate the stomach or get lodged in the mouth or throat.

• Resist the temptation to share your party treats with your cat; chocolate, for example, is toxic to these animals. Other celebration-time hazards are fireworks and constant streams of visitors for parties, and general stress. Keep your cat securely indoors and well away from the front door.

6

Because of a cat's inquisitive nature, you are likely to find your pet in all sorts of unusual places. Always check the washing machine and clothes' dryer before operating it in case your cat has chosen it for its bed.

POISONING

• Many over-the-counter human pain medications, e.g. aspirin, are toxic for cats as they lack the liver enzymes to digest them. Signs of accidental ingestion are salivation, vomiting and weakness. Do not give your own medicines to your cat and keep them somewhere safe where the cat can't get at them.

• Many flea insecticides are also toxic and will produce signs such as salivation, running eyes (lacrimation/tear production), vomiting, excess urination and diarrhoea. Bathe the cat in warm water with a drop of washing-up liquid to remove the flea product. Never use dog flea treatments on cats, as they can be toxic. Don't use sprays meant for the home or the garden on your pet. Try safe, non-toxic methods of controlling fleas—pyrethrins and d-limolene-based products are effective against fleas and safe for cats.

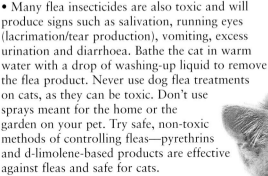

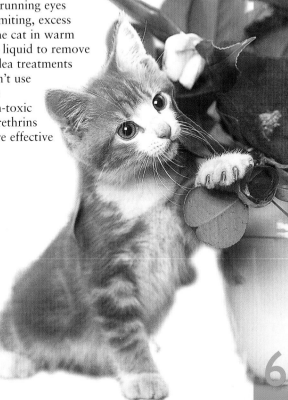

Warning

Some plants tend to find their way into the home at Christmas or other holidays.
The following are toxic although not usually seriously so:
Poinsettia (Euphorbia), Ivy and Mistletoe.

6

DANGERS IN THE GARDEN

Cats tend to wander far afield when you let them outside, so you will not be able to supervise them as closely as if they were in the home. Even so, by appreciating the potential dangers, not only will you be able to avoid them in your garden, but you can also be alert to the problems that may crop up and react appropriately.

PLANT HAZARDS

• Cats will normally chew plants, indoors and out, and will chew on grass and other plants deliberately to make themselves sick to get rid of hairballs. Some plants may also provide them with roughage and mineral and extra vitamins. However, there are plants that can be toxic, even fatal, and it is best to avoid having those plants in your garden.

• Toxic plants found outdoors include Taxus (Japanese yew). This contains a potentially fatal cardiac toxin and your cat may die of heart failure. Just one tenth of 1 percent of the cat's body weight can prove a fatal dose.

Rhododendrons, foxgloves and nightshades are also toxic—cats are mostly put off by their scents fortunately.

• Provide your cat with safe things to nibble on—herbs, such as parsley, or a catnip plant.

GARDEN HAZARDS

• Cats are likely to investigate barbecue debris and may pick up sharp pieces of bone or burn themselves on the barbecue itself. They will also rip open rubbish bags to get at smelly fragments and may encounter the cut edges of tins or broken glass.

6

If your cat is allowed to roam freely in your neighbourhood, there is little you can do to monitor its safety. You can, however, make your garden a safer place for it to be.

WINTERTIME HAZARDS

Winter brings special dangers for your pet, and special precautions are necessary to protect it.

• Cats hide in or under car engines to get warm and can be seriously if not fatally injured. Always blow your horn and tap on the bonnet before starting your car in winter.

• If your cat does not have access to clean, unfrozen water, it is likely to drink whatever it can find. This may include dangerous household chemicals or antifreeze. Antifreeze is particularly dangerous because its sweet smell appeals to cats. The active ingredient is ethylene glycol, which is toxic to the neurological system and kidneys. Signs of poisoning are depression, lack of coordination, vomiting and seizure. It is essential to get the cat to the vet immediately because it will be fatal if not caught within two hours of ingestion. Two teaspoons of it are enough to kill a cat.

• Keep any poison containers closed and well locked away. Clean up spills immediately and get rid of whatever you've used to mop up straight into the garbage bin.

6

HIT BY CAR

The increasing number of vehicles on the roads today means that the risk to cats is higher than ever. They are especially vulnerable for a number of reasons, including their habit of lurking under cars and leaping out at passing birds. If you suspect a cat has been hit by a car, or you see a cat being hit, a veterinary check-up is vital. Cats involved in car accidents may not show external signs of injury. The skin is resilient and may remain intact despite severe internal injuries.

Warning

Road accidents involving cats are more likely to happen at night when visibility is reduced, so it is preferable to keep your pet in at night. Try to develop a routine of getting a young kitten inside before dark. With luck, as it grows older, your cat will come back at this time unprompted.

CAUSES

• Cats appear to lack road sense. If a cat gets a sudden fright near a road, it will instinctively dart out across it, heedless of any danger.

• At night cats are blinded by bright headlights and will freeze on the spot. They are also extra susceptible in the breeding season, when they are ruled by their hormones. There is no way to train a cat to avoid roads, but you make you pet more obvious to drivers by giving it an elasticated collar with a reflective strip.

Cats have a habit of sitting under cars and dashing out unexpectedly into a road.

6

At night, when they are on the prowl, cats can easily be blinded by oncoming headlights, because of the reflective layer known as the tapetum lucidum at the back of their eyes.

WHAT YOU CAN DO

• Many cats are killed outright as the result of road collisions, but some survive unscathed. Even so, it is important to have your pet examined by a vet without delay, because there could be internal injuries, such as a ruptured spleen, which are serious and potentially life-threatening if undiagnosed. A cat that has had a lucky escape will still feel distressed and will need to be handled carefully.

• In order to take your cat to the vet, you need to pick it up and move it carefully. You can use a blanket, a sheet or even a towel to act as a small stretcher. Cover the cat by gently wrapping a blanket round it. Carry it to your car holding each end of the blanket or, if you have a board, slide the cat onto that without changing its position or bending its spine.

• Find a small sturdy box and gently place the cat in it, using no pillows as these will distort its body position.

• Your injured cat may bite you—a straightforward reaction to stress—so take care when handling it or cover its head with a towel.

• You should phone ahead and let your vet know that you are on your way. If it's an unusual hour, calling ahead ensures that the clinic is actually open.

• A cat may go into shock after being hit by a car—it will feel cold and its breathing will speed up. Try to keep the cat warm and comfortable until you reach the vet. If possible get someone to hold the cat while you drive.

6

CUTS, SCRAPES AND WOUND

Cats rarely suffer from superficial injuries to the skin, because their fur, especially the dense undercoat, provides a remarkably strong barrier. Barbed wire can be hazardous, however, ripping through the skin. Scratches as the result of fights sometimes occur, although, in comparison with abscesses that are caused by a bite that becomes infectious, they are rare.

WHAT YOU AND YOUR VET CAN DO

• Clean up round the wound with warm water, an iodine-type soap and cotton balls. Rinse again with water. Use clippers or scissors to remove the surrounding hair.

• Protect yourself when handling an injured cat. If you think it might bite you because it is hurt or scared, protect youself by wrapping its head in a towel. Don't leave the towel on for too long or wrap it too tightly.

• Assess the severity of the injury. If it is very deep, cover it as best you can with gauze, tape it in place and take the cat to the vet. If the wound does not look too bad, leave it bandaged till the morning, take the bandage off then and reassess it. The vet may prescribe antibiotics at this stage to prevent infection.

• Once the wound has formed a scab and healing is underway, there is still a risk of complications. About this time, the healing tissue starts to itch and the cat may then scratch off enough of the scab to cause the wound to bleed again. To prevent the cat aggravating a wound in this way, your vet may fit it with an Elizabethan collar—which most cats hate.

• Monitor the healing process. If the wound is not healing properly and your cat is showing other signs of illness, arrange to see your vet.

An Elizabethan collar will stop a cat from reaching the wound, but it won't be happy to wear it!

6

Cats always seem to have an admirable sense of balance, but because of their adventurous natures they will often injure themselves through climbing on fencing.

COMPLEMENTARY TREATMENTS

⊠ HERBAL REMEDIES

Calendula (Marigold) lotion, 6 drops in 30 ml (2 tbsp) of water, will reduce pain. Apply to the wound, cover with gauze, tape the gauze to itself.

Calendula-hypericum ointment applied to a minor wound will promote healing. Leave the wound open.

▢ HOMEOPATHIC REMEDIES

Calendula 6x is often recommended for superficial wounds. One tablet twice daily promotes healing.

Arnica decreases bruising.

If the wound becomes infected, *Hepar sulphuris* helps to expel pus.

Rescue Remedy will also aid recovery and reduce trauma.

6

FRACTURES

The most likely cause of fractured bones in cats is being hit by a car. There are three main types of fracture. A hairline fracture, in which the bone shows signs of a crack, will heal the most rapidly. In a so-called simple fracture, there is a clear break, with the bones still in close contact with each other. The most serious—and easiest to see—is a compound fracture in which part of the bone has been forced through the skin.

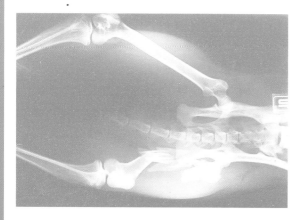

A shattered femur is evident in this X ray. This fracture will repair itself, but healing will take several weeks.

WHAT YOU AND YOUR VET CAN DO

• If you think your cat may have a broken bone, you need to get it to the vet as soon as possible. Follow the guidelines for moving an injured cat on page 105. Keep the broken limb or injured side uppermost, and supported if possible. The cat will probably be suffering from shock, so it is essential to keep it warm.

• If you think a leg is broken and you live a long way from a vet, you may have to make a splint. Use a couple of pieces of newspaper or a small towel. Wrap it round the fracture including the joint above and below the break and then secure it with tape. Do not attempt this unless it is strictly necessary.

• Your vet will take an X ray of the affected area, which is likely to entail giving an anaesthetic. It may be possible to set the fracture immediately.

• Limb fractures may be repaired by being encased in fibreglass or plaster casts, wiring, stainless steel pinning or plating.

• Adding a calcium supplement to your cat's food will ensure that there is no deficiency which could slow down the healing process.

6

ANIMAL ATTACKS

Cats are generally able to look after themselves in encounters with other animals but can occasionally receive wounds from dogs, foxes or even hedgehogs. The most likely source of injury, however, is from other cats, in territorial disputes either in the house or outdoors. It is often hard to locate puncture wounds in a cat's coat immediately after a fight with another cat. Feline AIDS and feline leukaemia are two diseases which can be transmitted during fights. Bite wounds are the major way in whch feline AIDS is spread. Your vet should do a blood test to check for these in your injured cat.

Warning

In many parts of the world, snake bites represent a hazard to cats, but unless you are present when your cat is bitten, the cause of its sudden collapse will be not be obvious. Emergency veterinary treatment is absolutely essential under these circumstances. If you do see a snake, but cannot identify it, write down a description, as this will make it easier for the vet to identify the snake and give the most effective treatment.

WHAT YOU AND YOUR VET CAN DO

• Cleaning wounds once or twice daily with hydrogen peroxide helps prevent infection. Some wounds heal cleanly, but abscesses (see p. 62) will develop in others.

• Abscesses usually take from 3–7 days to appear after a cat fight. Most need to be lanced, flushed and drained by your vet.

• Wasps, bees and other stinging insects (see p. 64) are a hazard in the summer months. Cats may find toads irresistible prey because they are slow moving and easy to catch. Once in the cat's mouth, however, the toxins from the toad's skin will cause it to start foaming, forcing the cat to drop it. You will need to flush out the cat's mouth with water, if at all possible, and then contact your vet for advice.

• Supplement the cat's diet with 250 mg vitamin C powder, added to the diet twice a day.

DROWNING

Although cats hate water, they are actually fairly good swimmers. They can, however, get into trouble by falling into water butts, swimming pools and garden ponds. Once trapped in a body of water with no easy way to get out, especially if the water level is well below the rim so it cannot haul itself out, the cat will soon become exhausted and will be at risk of drowning.

WHAT YOU AND YOUR VET CAN DO

• If you rescue a drowning cat, drastic action will be required, especially if it is hardly breathing. Hold the cat up by its hind legs, just above the joint hocks, and gently swing it from side to side to remove the water from the lungs. When you lay the cat down, keep its head slightly lower than its body if possible and check there is no obstruction of the airway. Then lay the cat on its right side and massage the chest with gentle pressure, which should help to ensure that it keeps breathing.

• If you are certain that the cat is breathing normally, rub it briskly down with a towel—after its experience it may be chilled, or even in shock. Keep the cat warm and quiet. If you are in any doubt about its recovery, do not hesitate to get veterinary advice.

6

USEFUL ADDRESSES

BRITISH HOLISTIC VETERINARY MEDICAL ASSOCIATION
Mrs Sue Thomas
The Croft,
Tockwith Road,
Longmarston,
Yorks YO26 7PQ
Association of qualified veterinary practitioners with skills in complementary therapies. Write for details of practitioners in your area.

BRITISH HOMEOPATHIC ASSOCIATION
27a Devonshire Street,
London W1N 1RJ
tel: 0207 935 2163
Can provide a list of medically qualified homeopathic vets.

ROYAL COLLEGE OF VETERINARY SURGEONS
62–64 Horseferry Road,
London SW1P 2AF
tel: 0207 222 2001
fax: 0207 222 2004
http://www.rcvs.org.uk/rcvs/
UK statutory body for the veterinary profession. Can provide a list of veterinary surgeons in your area. Information about pet problems may be obtained from the website.

ALTERNATIVE VETERINARY MEDICINE CENTRE
Chinham House
Stanford in the Vale
Faringdon
Oxon SN7 8NQ
tel: 01367 710 324
fax: 01367 718 243
Holds list of alternative medical practitioners specializing in holistic treatment.

GOVERNING COUNCIL OF THE CAT FANCY
4–6 Penel Orlieu, Bridgwater,
Somerset TA6 3PG
tel: 01278 427 575
fax: 01278 446 627
http://ourworld.compuserve.com/homepages/GCCF_CATS
Registration organization to which UK cat clubs are affiliated.

CATS PROTECTION
17 Kings Road, Horsham,
West Sussex RH13 5PP
tel: 01403 221 900
helpline: 01403 221 919
A charity which has local groups, provides general advice on rescue, rehousing and neutering.

BLUE CROSS
Field Centre, Shilton Road,
Burford,
Oxford OX18 4PF
tel: 01993 822651
fax: 01993 823 083
Animal charity which relies on donations to provide free veterinary care for animals in low-income families. Has adoption centres for animals needing new homes.

WWW HOMEPAGES
http://www.altvetmed.com
AltVetMed – general alternative medicine

http://www.naturalholistic.com
Natural Holistic Pet Care

http://www.med.auth.gr/~karanik/english/veter.htm
Veterinary Acupuncture Page

6

INDEX

ACKNOWLEDGMENTS

PICTURE CREDITS: t = top, b = bottom, l = left, r = right, c = centre

1-5, 7l, 9, 38-40t, 41, 43t, 44l, 52t, 56r, 57l, 63, 65, 70, 85t, 87, 92b, 93t, 96b, 111 David King; 6, 102 Sally Anne Thompson/Animal Photography; 7r, 18b, 75 David Jordan; 8t, 21, 46b, 49r, 59b Iain Bagwell; 8b, 13b,17b, 23b, 24l, 27tr, c, b, 29l, r, 31, 33l, 35b, 40b, 43b, 45, 51l, 52br, 55b, 56l, 57r, 69, 71, 85b, 93b Andrew Sydenham; 11, 33r, 36, Renee Stockdale/Oxford Scientific Films; 12 Andrew Linscott/RSPCA Photolibrary; 13r, 14, 26, 27tl, 48l, 50l, 60, 61, 68, 72, 81, 83, 84, 86, 88, 91, 94, 98, 99, 106 Jane Burton; 16, 18t, 24r, 30, 54t, 77, 80r, 90 Jane Burton/Bruce Coleman Collection; 17t Animals Animals/Oxford Scientific Films; 20, 35t 42, 54b, 67, John Daniels; 23t, 28, 62, 64, 95, 96t, 109 Jane Burton/Warren Photographic; 25, 32 Animals Unlimited; 34, 52bl, 78, 79 Bradley Viner; 37 Daniel Valla/Oxford Scientific Films; 44r Tina Carvalho/Oxford Scientific Films; 46t, 48r, John Mason/Ardea; 49l George I. Bernard/Oxford Scientific Films; 50r Science Photo Library; 51r, 101t Richard Packwood/Oxford Scientific Films; 55t Marc Henrie; 58, 103, 107, 110 Hans Reinhard/Bruce Coleman Collection; 59r Judith Platt/RSPCA Photolibrary; 66 Kim Taylor/Bruce Coleman; 73 London Scientific Films/Oxford Scientific Films; 74 CNRI/Science Photo Library; 80l David Barron/Oxford Scientific Films; 82 Clem Haagner/Ardea; 89, 104 Angela Hampton/RSPCA Photolibrary; 92t, 97, 100, 101b John Daniels/Ardea; 105 Konrad Wothe/Oxford Scientific Films; 108 Dorling Kindersley